Your Seat Cushion Is A Flotation Device

and other buoyant short stories

PRISCILLA

GRACIAS POR

HACERME SENTIR EN

FAMILIA.

"Nada está perdido si se tiene el valor de proclamar que todo está perdido y que hay que empezar de nuevo."

Nothing is lost if we have the courage to proclaim that all is lost and that we must begin again.

— Julio Cortazar

To Kathia.
You give me more than you will ever
know.

Author's Note:

Any reference to time across the book, "a month ago, a week ago", respects when the essay was written.

Contents

I Hid The Broccoli

When I was little I would try to hide things from my parents.

Junk food. The broccoli I had to finish, strategically buried under the rice. My report card.

I always got caught.

One day my mom, who in her words *"has eyes in the back of her head"*, didn't notice my tongue was bright purple. I had been eating a grape popsicle and tried to rinse out my mouth but the color wouldn't come out.

I went to bed considering how not getting caught made me feel. Doing something I was told not to do, with no one to witness it.

I expected I would feel free. Instead, my purple tongue bothered me.

I realized that even though no one had seen it, I had seen it.

I would always be watching me.

That's when I first articulated that the best version of me was a constant witness to the other me. The one who loses her patience. The one who gets angry at things that don't matter. The one who takes the path of least resistance, who cuts corners, who is lazy. The one who resorts to white lies.

The one who knows something no one else would ever detect: all the times I'm not doing my best.

I don't like how it feels for one part of me to be out of sync with the other. Fragmented, inconsistent. I like cohesion.

I strive every day for all of me to be like the best of me.

Why Do We Fall Out Of Love?

He'll move away and you'll try to stay in touch at first but then you won't.

He'll say he needs space and then come back but it will be too late.

He needed space and so your heart sent him to Saturn.

Because he lied and swore he wasn't cheating on you. You'll explain that what mattered was the lie, what matters is the truth, and he will repeat over and over that he didn't cheat.

Even your fight is about two separate things.

Because at first you thought his silence was enigmatic but it turns out he had nothing to say.

You interpreted what he did as a form of betrayal even if it wasn't and you can't move past your own interpretation of his actions and no longer feel safe.

He will want you to be different. And at first you try but eventually you being exhausted crowds out you being in love.

Because he lied and the lie was insignificant. He can't believe you are leaving for something so small but it's not what he lied about.

It's that he can no longer be the person you were certain would never lie to you.

You will write him a poem and he will read it and ask you to *explain* it to him.

You fall out of love for every reason.

You fall out of love for no reason.

Why Do We Fall In Love?

I think maybe it was his toes. They are crooked and splay out in a way I find supremely endearing.

Or how he sleeps, so deep and so still, snoring like a cartoon bear.

How he chops, like a professional. He takes several carrots at a time and in a noisy blur turns them into uniform orange disks.

He loves to cook, uses the word "caramelize" and assures me bacon is a condiment.

He came with a large, cumbersome espresso machine — he will only use a French press as a last resort — and a trunk full of Inuit art.

I had never met anyone who owned a sculpture created to protect us.

Whenever I act unreasonable, which is often, he looks at me both irritated and in disbelief.

At my most indignant I amuse him.

How can anyone be this annoying? (And by "anyone" I mean me.)

He only wears black boots and white button down shirts and has grey hair.

Now that I think about it, it was the grey hair.

He's even-keeled, gruff, gritty and often curmudgeonly. I don't drink. He drinks Manhattans.

He gives me fashion advice.

Me: *"I love these boots but I won't buy them because I will never wear them."*

Him: *"They go with everything you own and you'll wear them every day. Besides, you can't decline yellow lace-ups."*

I wear them every day.

He smells good.

I fell in love with him because he smells good.

Every time we went out he would be there already, waiting for me. On our very first date I had dinner and he only had a drink and he insisted on paying, despite my protests.

He was always direct. He told the truth. He doesn't mince words. (*"Did you miss me while you were at work?" "No. Not really."*)

After dating for a little over two months I told him he needed to fly to Mexico to meet my family. I thought he'd balk. He didn't.

I fell in love with him because he calls his Mom regularly and spends hours on the phone with his sister.

Because he does things I'd rather he didn't and I can't stop him.

We fall in love for every reason. We fall in love for no reason.

Things I Believe In That I Know Aren't True

When I was in my early twenties a dog walked into my life and I called her Joy and I will never love anything quite like I loved her.

It was because of her that I became a rescued person.

She died many years ago and I still miss her and I believe that when I die she will welcome me into heaven, with her wide pitbull smile and broad white chest.

I believe I was the most wanted baby on the planet.

Ever since I can remember my Mom has told me stories about how my parents could not have children and then, against all odds, I came along.

More recently I have found out things that don't completely add up to this fairy tale of my improbable, triumphant arrival but it's too late. It's already a part of my composition.

Speaking of my Mom she is in her 80s and a force of nature. I believe she is indestructible.

On the days I concede no one is immortal I believe she will one day gallop off into the desert on a black Arabian horse.

I believe that my Dad, who died a year ago, is still here with me.

Even better, I believe that somewhere there is an alternate universe where he is still young and I am still a little girl. Somewhere he is still holding my hand as I run across the sand.

I believe I have an army of guardian angels.

I believe everything is going to be OK.

I don't know if there is a God. I don't know what happens after we die. I don't know if there is a heaven.

I believe in many things I know aren't true (or suspect might not be true) and figure that, since nobody really knows, my beliefs are as good as any.

The Last

Boyfriend and I were walking along Baker Beach.

It was very cold that day and the beach looked almost deserted.

We kissed.

"Wow!" I said. *"That was the very first time I ever kissed anyone on Baker Beach!"*

"That doesn't matter," he said. *"What I want is to be the last."*

Hungry

I am hungry for words

for learning more about myself

for books

a glass of cold water

not for tricky territory

or moving pieces across a flimsy chessboard

not for inattention or cunning

for order

a floor polished clean

for clarity and light

for a tide pool

for beauty

and a new lined notebook

Fussy Boy

Many years ago my mother, my brother and I were walking around in a mall.

I must have been around 8, which means my brother must have been 6.

Suddenly, we heard a kid screaming his head off.

"Children," my Mom says, almost muttering to herself, *"listen to that child. Those are not normal cries of a fussy boy. That is the sound of a terrified, desperate kid in absolute, indescribable distress. Something terrible is — OH MY GOD OH MY GOD DUSHKA WHERE IS YOUR BROTHER?"*

He was on the other side of the makeup counter.

Things I Avoid

I avoid certainty. It's a liar.

I avoid safety. It's a fallacy.

I avoid danger. If it can happen to others, it can happen to me.

I avoid elliptical discussions. I have outgrown the imperative to convince anyone of anything.

I avoid crowds, noise, and loud and aggressive people. These things pointlessly agitate me.

I avoid promises. In a turbulent world they are rarely viable.

I avoid leaving things unsaid.

I avoid anything I only feel lukewarm about, and anything insipid. Salt. Salt the narrative, the possibilities, your expectations and the oven-roasted vegetables.

I avoid clutter and imposed complexity.

I avoid forcing design on an accident.

I avoid frivolity, despair and disconnection. These are all symptoms of an indolent imagination.

I avoid believing anything is determined.

I avoid scratchy sweaters.

Easy To Love

I have a friend, Jon, who has three children. He always speaks of the middle one, Vanessa. He tells me a lot about her and rarely talks about the other two.

"Jon," I ask him one day. *"Do you have a favorite child?"*

He considers this.

"No," he says. *"I love them all very differently, but the same."*

"I always thought Vanessa was your favorite."

He smiles. *"It's not that she's my favorite. It's that she's easier to love."*

My Year In Europe

My Dad was very conservative, very strict, and very, very apprehensive.

When I was growing up he insisted on personally meeting all my friends. Curfews were harsh and enforced. He had zero tolerance for disobedience. Many, many things were forbidden: sleepovers, getting up late on weekends, bad grades.

When I turned 17 and was months away from finishing high school, I decided I would ask if I could spend a year in Europe, traveling and learning French.

I knew full well there was absolutely no chance he would agree.

He said yes. He didn't hesitate.

My Dad died about a year ago and I recently found a box filled with all the letters we wrote to each other during my year abroad. (This was 1987. There was no Internet and long distance calls were so expensive we spoke once a month.)

Every letter I write is filled with wonder. I frequent museums and read books and walk along the Seine.

I tell him I cannot believe the world is so beautiful and thank him for giving it to me. *"I feel every day like you wrapped Paris up for me."*

He asks if I am learning French. He insists that I read as much as I can. He requests that I write letters to him while sitting in sidewalk cafes.

He makes book recommendations. *"Read Rilke,"* he instructs. *"Read Sartre and Simone de Beauvoir in their original language. Read Hemingway. A lot of what he wrote he wrote when he was living in Paris."*

In one letter I ask him why he isn't inquiring about my behavior. Why has he never asked if I am staying up late, if I am going out at night? Does he not wonder if I have a French boyfriend?

"My work related to your decision-making is done," he writes. *"At this point all I can do is hope I did a good job. The rest is up to you."*

I ask him too if he worries about me. *"I worry every day,"* he says. *"But we don't raise children to keep them by us forever."*

This was the first time my father let me go. I can tell you now, decades later, that that year in Europe was formative for me. In a fortunate happy life, it's one of the best things that ever happened to me.

RAWR

I saw it in the guy at the gym who did four handstand push-ups with perfect form.

In the mixologist at the bar, concocting each drink with the precision of a chemist.

In the plumber who carried a crescent wrench and knew how to use it.

In the poet and the perfect rhythm of his verses.

In my yoga teacher and his beautifully balanced Natarajasana.

It will get me every time, like an arrow straight through my heart.

Competence. Hot.

Around The Universe

Boyfriend: *"I love you."*

Me: *"Yeah? How much?"*

Boyfriend: *"About this much."*

He places his index finger close to his thumb.

Me: *"Whah?"*

Him: *"My love isn't the distance from my index finger to my thumb. It's the distance from my index finger all around the universe and back to my thumb."*

I was considering what I could do to close the distance between his thumb and index finger when an astronomer told me that *"we have measured the curvature of the universe, and it is very close to not curved at all."*

"If it is curved," Lynnie Saade explains, *"it seems to be more likely open, due to its accelerating expansion."*

"Both these cases mean you can't end up right back where you started by "going around" the cosmos, as there's no "around"."

It stands to reason then that Boyfriend's love is infinite.

Pack My Bag

In my second job ever my boss and I traveled from Mexico City to San Diego for an important new business pitch.

The meeting ran much longer than we expected.

I had my small overnight bag with me so was ready to go directly from the meeting to the airport.

We walked down to the building lobby and my boss handed me his room key.

"Please return to the hotel," he said. *"Go up to my room and pack my bag, then take a later flight."*

He took a taxi right to the airport and had no bags to carry.

I went back to the hotel, packed all his personal belongings including dirty underwear, changed my flight, checked both bags and did not arrive home until much later.

I'm glad I came across him early in my career so I could learn as early as possible everything I needed to know about setting boundaries.

The Beginning

The law of conservation of energy states that it is neither created nor destroyed, only transformed.

It stands to reason then that my feelings are not recent.

There were elements of their chemical composition in solar nebula and in the supernova explosion that created our planet.

In the marine vapour of asteroids that collided and became salt water, which poured into crevasses, filling them with vital fluid that aided in the creation of species that have not yet been discovered.

They were there during the trace of the wide, blue curve of the sky. The clear, straight line of the horizon. The puzzle-like composition of our continents.

There were particles of it in the ink the Gods used when they wrote that book, the one that determines the fate of every one of us.

We could infer then that my feelings were there before the existence of nostalgia. Before any emblem. Before religion. Before the inception of our internal labyrinths. Before our most cherished, most valuable, most primal memories.

Before the formation of the ash they claim we come from.

It was there during the perfect design of coiled fern leaves, before the geometric pattern of turtle shells.

In one of those cases of temporal ellipsis we could detect evidence of it today in the dust that covers the fossils found in glass cases across every natural history museum.

In time he and I will get to know each other better. We will give space to this current version of us.

But, as you can see, it already doesn't matter.

It doesn't matter, because way after we no longer are whatever we will become, this energy will continue to exist, its molecules stable, intact, free, disperse; maybe lending cobwebs their glimmer. Maybe responsible for the shade of green in new grass.

We'll see its flicker in the stars that some day someone will connect into another anonymous constellation or in the evidence of a love story that, like everything, has existed always.

Flowers

After a tumultuous marriage and a difficult divorce my Dad sent my Mom flowers every year on my birthday and would then call her to thank her for making me.

He did this every year from the day I was born until the day he died.

How Do You Know If Someone Is For Real?

I know he's for real because on our very first date he was interested.

I don't mean interested in dating me. I mean interested in me.

That same night he called me a few minutes after I got home. I found it so refreshing that he couldn't be bothered with playing games.

Since that day he follows through on what he says he's going to do and shows up when he says he will. He always calls when he'll be late.

It's not just that he's reliable. It's that he's steady.

I know he is for real because he has seen me at my worst and he's still here.

Because my father, who could see right through anyone, told me what he was. *A solid character.*

I know he's for real because he's there for others, not just for me. He has friends he's known since he was a kid but also new friends he's met through me.

I know he's for real because he's close to my family, and his.

He has this clock that used to belong to his Dad. It was important for him to get it in working condition even though nobody needs a clock to know what time it is anymore.

One day, back when we first met, I told him about my divorce. I briefly mentioned that the saddest I ever felt was alone in a supermarket parking lot with a cart full of food, wondering how it was that at 42 I had no one to carry the bags with.

We've been together four years and when we come home from the grocery store I insist I'm far from helpless. I tell him it wasn't really about carrying the bags. I tell him I'm happy to take one or two, but stubborn that he is he insists on grabbing every single one.

Hugged By A Stranger On The Bus

On bus:

Girl 1: *"If he says he's not ready to move in, he's not that into you."*

Girl 2: *"What if he's just not ready to move in?"*

Me: *"There's a way to tell."*

Girl 2: *"Tell!"*

Me: *"Is he there for you in other ways?"*

Girl 2: *"Yes."*

Me: *"I know you want him to want to move in. But are you ready to move in?"*

Girl 2: *"Hmmm."*

Me: *"Are you into him, yet think you should wait a bit?"*

Girl 2: *"Yes."*

Me: *"Then so is he."*

And that is how I was hugged by a stranger on the bus.

Oh, Italy

Italy was not a unified country until very recently.

In fact, after many trips to Italy I can say with confidence that there is no such thing as "Italian Food". Or, rather, the range of food that can be considered "Italian" varies so much from region to region that it defies categorization.

In Liguria I dreamed of bread and with good reason.

Camogli is on the coast close to Genova, and it was so hot I slept with the windows open.

The drool inducing smell from the *panetteria* below rises, wafts through the open window and seeps into your subconscious. They start work at 3:00 a.m. I don't need to tell you what you wake up craving for.

Liguria is where *focaccia* comes from, as well as *troffie, pesto, sugo di noce, moscardini in umido, pesce in umido con patate bollite.* We had *gelato* at least three times a day (after lunch, early evening and after dinner).

Good friends took us by boat from Camogli to San Fruttuoso for dinner one evening. On the way we saw Liguria from the water, its nooks and soft lights.

I remember reading somewhere that when you cook pasta the water needs to be as salty as the Mediterranean, so I tasted it. Next time I'll get it right.

We sat at a little table right on the beach, eating a seven course meal under the light of the moon.

After the coast, we went by bus up to the mountains to a small town called Etroubles.

Whenever we visited Etroubles (which has approximately 200 inhabitants and is close to the border with Switzerland), my now ex-husband felt like a time traveler.

The same six-year-old girl who used to sit behind the counter at the grocery store when he was twelve is still there, with her tangled red head, counting coins.

Except that, on closer inspection, it was the daughter of the girl that used to be there.

This phenomenon repeats itself as we walk through town in the boy on the swings, the teenagers playing soccer, the woman hanging her clothes to dry.

The food in Valle d'Aosta is stick to your ribs, rich, heavy, and slathered in butter, cream or cheese. *Polenta e Camoscio, Polenta Concia, Fonduta, Mocetta, Zuppa alla Valpellinese, Tegole, Carpaccio di Porcini*. I had *Zuppa alla Valpellinese* and found myself in front of a deep dish of melted *Fontina*, which I then spread on thick, black bread with my fork. (You'd think *"zuppa"* would require a spoon. I love surprises.)

In Courmayeur, at the foot of *Monte Bianco (Mont Blanc)*, I had the best yogurt I've ever tasted. The label on the glass container read "this yogurt is made only from milk of cows from the high Valle d'Aosta". As we drove through the mountains, I thanked all the cows who grazed there.

My ex husband is from Lombardia (Milan). Typical Milan dishes are *Risotto alla Milanese* (which is made with saffron), *Osso Buco* (which I admit I'm not a passionate fan of — but all around me people mop their plate clean with bread), *Cotoletta alla Milanese* (breaded meat which even in far away places like Mexico we call "Milanesa") and *Panettone*, the high, fluffy, dried fruit encrusted dessert bread sold in Milan over the Christmas holidays.

I know that my initial declaration of there being no such thing as Italian food is really nothing new. It's that it's such fun to experience it for oneself.

Stand Tall

I am 5'5".

The only time I have been unhappy with my height I was 16 and dating a guy who was shorter than me.

He constantly berated me for *"not being dainty"* and demanded that I never wear anything other than absolutely flat shoes.

I am so glad I met him. He taught me early on how empty, futile and preposterous it is to try to change who we are; how absurd it is to diminish ourselves in an effort to please another person.

Thank you, wherever you are, for teaching me how to stand tall.

Gone Forever

When I was very young, grown-ups used to tell me that those years that I was living would be the most wonderful of my life. And I would think *No way. You can't possibly be right.*

The future would always be better, whatever was in store for me, and I couldn't wait for it to start.

I see their point now. I don't think I realized at the time what they were really trying to say: that what I was experiencing then would one day very soon be irretrievable.

I will never again come home and hear my mother furiously typing downstairs.

I will never walk into the dining room at my father's house and find all my brothers and sisters sitting at the table in their pajamas, their energy, their kinetic force, dark hair disheveled, my sister still a baby.

My father, so very young, the fire in his eyes, his brow furrowed, sitting behind his desk at the library, surrounded by books in piles that were taller than me.

Things have splintered since then, and we've all scattered in different directions and built very different lives.

If I had the choice to go back even for a day, an hour, I don't think I'd want to. I like it so much better here.

But I feel anyway that I've lost something enormous.

No Matter What

I wonder

at the very end

what will remain

If Boyfriend

or a family member

or my work

or a friend

or my house

or a book

or a recipe

or what I haven't done

but that I plan to do

or someone I haven't even met

I wonder how the sentence

I will use for consolation

will conclude

because at the very least

no matter what

I will still have my _____

Happiness Is Elusive

Every so often I am overwhelmed by a feeling of well being.

And then I wonder if "well being" does a good job describing it.

It's not a rush, like joy or enthusiasm (which fortunately I'm also prone to). It's softer and fuller. Should I call it "Wellness"? Nah. Too clinical. This is more akin to fulfillment, to (dare I say it?) happiness.

Maybe it just needs a bit of Italian flair. *Benessere*.

Or, Greek. *Eudaimonia*.

The point is that, regrettably, I've come to discover that it's not a feeling I can chase. It has to come on its own. I can't find it in good meals, in conversations with friends or the company of people I love. It's not in a spa, even if the massage was a particularly good one. It doesn't present itself when I buy new shoes, or finalize a good document. It doesn't hold hands with the (delightful) sense of a job well done. It's unpredictable. It always surprises me.

It shows up quietly, say, when I travel and am surrounded by unfamiliar sights, smells, sounds. But it doesn't come on every trip.

It arrives when I'm sitting somewhere, not making an effort to do three things at once. When I'm just taking the world in.

But if I tell myself to focus on staying in the present and just enjoying the moment for what it is, it evades me.

Is this what happiness is? An elusive, ephemeral tease of a feeling that you can't consciously go after?

It might be my inalienable right to pursue it, but if I do, I might miss it entirely.

First Love

His name was Fritz. He was Norwegian. He had blond hair and eyes so blue I felt I could see the inner workings of his thoughts.

I plotted accidental encounters.

He completely, utterly ignored me. This was not an active effort. He truly did not know I existed.

Sometimes, I extended thoughtful love offerings (mostly snacks) and looked at him adoringly. His reaction was absolute perplexity.

Once, early one morning I gathered all my courage, walked over to him and said *"Hola!"* (hello in Spanish) to which he frowned and replied *"Hola."*

I analyzed his tone, cadence and inflection for days.

One day, months before the official end of the school year, I walked into class and noticed his desk was empty. The teacher told me he and his parents had moved back to Norway.

He was gone.

I never saw him again.

Both Fritz and I must have been five or six years old.

Childless

A few years ago a friend came to spend some time with me in California.

He and his three children, ages 8, 11 and 14, stayed at my house for a few days.

It was a fascinating experience, sociologically speaking.

When I was a kid I solemnly swore I'd never, ever be like a grown-up. I wrote this sacred vow across the top page of my diary. In fact, the diary itself was meant as a reminder to a future me; inoculation against whatever it was that possessed adults, causing them to forget all that was important.

It took me 2 seconds flat to turn into my parents.

I put these kids on a regimented schedule so I could holler *"Time for breakfast! Time for a bath! Bed time!"* and, my personal favorite *"No, not in two minutes. Now!"*

I said *"shhhh!"* a lot. I made them eat their fruit and vegetables before they could open bags of chips or eat cookies. To their whiny *"But, whyyy?"* I'd quickly retort *"Because I say so."*

In my defense, kids are noisy. They yell, opine, scream, complain, bang, weigh in, listen to (atrocious) music, and thump around like elephants.

They are chaotic. They each have different requirements and demands (Hot milk. Cold milk. Strawberry cereal. Banana without the mushy part. Can I please have some conditioner? My hair is all tangly!).

They are crazy expensive. They are perpetually thirsty, hungry and needy. I usually shop for two people who don't eat a whole lot. We struggle to finish a liter of milk in a week. With three kids in the house (and an extra adult), I bought milk by the gallon. They went through a dozen bananas a day. Boxes of cereal. One day, I made chocolate chip cookies (big hit) and they were gone before the cookie sheet had a chance to cool off.

I'm just glad they left before I needed to start worrying about cars, college educations and weddings.

Kids are messy (and smelly). The youngest one had the habit of walking around the house while dragging her sticky hands across the wall. A straw was inserted somewhat heartily into the apple juice, sending apple juice squirting all over counters, floors and chairs. Their shoes smell of feet (and so did the entrance to the house, since everyone left shoes there).

These creatures. Never. Get. Tired. After taking in their energy and bounciness I determined that the best course of action was to take them outside. We went to the beach. Played basketball. Went for a hike. Walked the dog. Had a picnic. Went bowling. They were still bouncy on the way back home. And woke up the next morning hungry again, bouncy again, needy again. As Joan Cusack so eloquently put it: *"The thing about kids is that they just keep coming at you."*

I was very happy to share my time and space with these amazing characters, but was equally happy to supervise their packing and departure.

Easter Belongs To You

Easter will forever belong to my mother's husband.

We used to wake up every Easter Sunday (we're not Catholic) and run out to the garden to find dozens of eggs.

They weren't chocolate (my brother was severely allergic to it). They were plastic, and I would unwrap and open them to find treasures inside: multicolored candy, sure, but other things too. Jewelry and miniature furniture, secret notes and toys.

It wasn't until years later that I realized he had to go look for things small enough to fit into the eggs, individually wrap them, get up early to hide them, and then put them away for the following year.

I am grateful to him for the role he has played in making my life a pastel colored place.

You know, the kind where you expect to find nestled in the grass a baby blue egg with a unicorn inside.

Skydiver

I jumped out of an airplane to impress I guy I was into.

I happened to mention one day my theory about vertigo. *"When I look down from very high up,"* I told him *"it doesn't feel like I'm afraid of heights. It feels like I want to jump. Not to die. To fly."*

"We should jump then."

What an excellent idea.

What could possibly go wrong?

We took a skydiving course required for those who intended to jump alone rather than tandem.

It took three months of daily exercise and "conditioning" to respond quickly and automatically, even under insane amounts of stress.

I showed up every day for the strenuous repetitive drills, assuring myself I could back out at any time.

And then there I was, standing on the wing of an airplane.

"Fall back!" shouted the instructor. *"Your body knows what to do."*

My body was freaking out.

As I fell I tossed around in wild circles before I could arch my back and cactus my arms out and stabilize myself and then I saw the entire arch of the sky like a bird.

It felt like the whole world was still and all the falling was happening in my stomach.

I am going to die.

I felt sad.

How could you? How could you be this stupid?

When my altimeter beeped I yanked my parachute open and felt like I was falling up, hard. I floated down to Earth far from where I was supposed to but close enough to walk back.

Once my feet touched the ground I was high on elation and massive amounts of adrenaline. I learned nothing that day.

I can tell you now, years later, that when I jumped out of that plane I had no clue what I was doing.

That the sensation was so startlingly different to what I expected that I have no idea how I had the presence of mind to open my parachute.

The army of guardian angels I believe look after me was working double time that day.

I make sure now to give them as much time off as possible, since I am still and will be forever in their debt.

Last Resort

When I was little and we got into his car my Dad told me that pressing the button on the hand brake would make the vehicle fly and that he only used it under duress as it was very, very dangerous.

Back then I half knew he was teasing but now, when I am stuck in awful traffic, I gently graze the button with my thumb and tell myself it's always there for me in case I need to deploy it as a very last resort.

What Are You Wearing?

A guy who used to work for me said he and his wife could pick me up at my house so we could drive to an office party together.

About an hour before they were supposed to arrive I got a text from him.

"Love — what are you wearing? Would you like me to bring you a dress?"

I read it twice before realizing he obviously meant to send it to his wife and not to me.

He was mortified.

I would not have teased him about it if I had known what awaited me.

Two weeks later he was supposed to come into my office for a meeting.

A call I was on was longer than I expected; I texted him so he wouldn't be standing at my door waiting for me to hang up the phone.

"Wait for me to call you. I need sex."

What I actually wrote was *"Wait for me to call you. I need a sec."*

Thank you, autocorrect.

I'll never live that one down.

Abraham

I have insomnia and suffer frequently from sleep paralysis, a terrifying condition where you feel you are awake but cannot move or speak. Sometimes I have trouble breathing.

I try to wake myself up — or try to move — and it's impossible.

I tell myself I will suffer less if I remain calm.

In this state, I almost always feel like other hostile people are in the room (which makes remaining calm impossible).

If you look up "sleep paralysis", this sense of someone else being present is reported by many people who have experienced this condition, which I find oddly comforting.

Last night I was waiting for Boyfriend to come home and he texted to let me know he'd be later than expected. I fell asleep on the couch.

Sleep paralysis set in and I felt the presence of a man standing behind me.

Unable to speak I thought *"Go away. My boyfriend will be home soon."*

"Tell him it's Abraham," he replied.

If you have ever experienced sleep paralysis I don't have to tell you how real this feels.

I managed to wake myself up (or recover my ability to move) and was still peeling the nightmare off me when Boyfriend walked in.

"Thank God you are home," I said. *"I had a terrible, vivid nightmare. I felt the presence of a man in the room. He said to tell you it was Abraham."*

"Oh," Boyfriend said. *"Abraham was my grandfather."*

Sweet Potatoes

I recently bought a couple of sweet potatoes with the intention of slicing them and baking them.

I placed them on my dining room table in a dry colander.

I know now I will never cook them because they are *sprouting.*

They have no earth and no water, despite of which the leaves are getting bigger every day.

They remind me so much of the times I have seen flowers growing out of cracks on the sidewalk.

Tenacious, ferocious, unrelenting.

I think life is beautiful.

I Like Your Tie

I met him at a global company meeting. He worked in the Milan office.

I walked up to him and told him I liked his tie.

I didn't know that doing so would alter the course of my life.

That marked the beginning of an unlikely long distance relationship. He was working in Italy. I was working in Mexico.

Because we were both employed by the same company, we did our best to keep our developing romance under wraps.

That was when the CEO called us and asked us if we wanted to start a life in California.

He needed two senior people to work on the Apple account and it would give our relationship the space it deserved.

We immediately said yes. We left our countries, our families, our friends and our way of life.

We started from scratch. Found an apartment. Built a team, then another. Bought a house.

The day we got married I knew with certainty he was the one.

We were married 15 years. We were an extraordinary team and incredibly good, supportive friends but when it came to the marriage part of the equation we felt increasingly unsatisfied and trapped.

We got an amicable divorce and remain extremely close to this day.

I never imagined I would divorce him.

If I could go back in time I would again tell him I liked his tie.

I'd again bet my life on that relationship, say yes on a bluff overlooking the Pacific Ocean, read on our red sofa and look at the moon through the skylight at the top of the stairs.

We'd again hold hands in that dreary divorce court and I would again know that beyond words like "marriage" or "divorce", we choose the people who are to be part of our life forever.

Never Late

When I was growing up I was extremely reliable. If I told either one of my parents I was arriving at midnight I would be home at midnight on the dot.

In my entire life I was only late once. There was an accident on the highway and I got home about two hours after I said I would (This was before cell phones existed).

When I got to my house there were two police cars outside. The policemen were talking to my Dad.

I walked up to him and his knees buckled when he saw me.

"You are NEVER late," he said as I explained. *"You are never late so I was sure something terrible had happened."*

I don't think I will ever forget that night. It's not that he was mad at me or that he was trying to make me feel bad. It's that I could see plain as day that I put him through hell.

I would never deliberately worry someone I love.

Why Bookcases Exist

I buy books all the time. I don't always read them.

I suspect I am not the only one. If I was, bookcases would not exist.

The books I buy do not imply a promise of immediate consumption.

Rather, they reveal an interest. Concern, involvement. Curiosity.

All essential ingredients to both success and happiness.

When I walk into my house and see my bookcases, the books stacked by my bed, on my window sill and coffee table, I do not think they are something I need to get done.

I think they are a gift to myself, to the person inside me who is restless and eager to learn something new.

I know too that even if I don't read them for a long time they will be there patiently waiting for me.

Incidentally, I do the same with notebooks. I buy them even when I don't immediately need them and ogle the soft, beautifully lined blank pages inside.

Some day they will be filled with my writing. I can't wait for that day. It's perfectly acceptable that it won't be today, or any time this week. Not even this year.

Miserable

I just spent a little under a week with my brother and his kids.

Kids are exhausting. When I spend time with them I wonder how parents ever get anything done.

These beasts are like freight trains, unstoppable, relentless, inquisitive.

They take everything out of you.

After a few days of hanging out with them I feel completely exasperated and overextended and look forward to going back to my quiet apartment.

I pack my dirty clothes (somehow covered in glitter and chalk) and hop into a car and feel free and then I cry all the way to the airport.

I miss them so.

It's Cancelled

Every Spanish speaking country speaks Spanish but pronunciation, cadence and even word usage vary (similar to "apartment" in the US and "flat" in the UK).

By way of example, I am Mexican and just spent a week in Colombia.

The word Mexicans use for "cancelled" (cancelado) in Colombia means "paid for". Every time I tried to pay for something they assured me it had been cancelled.

The word Mexicans use for now (ahora) in Colombia means "later."

Would you like some coffee?

Yeah, now.

Would you like milk in it?

No, no. Now.

Being a Spanish speaker and traveling to other Spanish speaking countries is delightful and lends itself to wonderful stories.

It also makes you appreciate just how often we are all probably misunderstanding each other.

To Do List

I want to be happy.

I want to be good. A good daughter, a good girlfriend, a good friend, a good co-worker. I wouldn't measure this their way. I would measure it mine.

I'd like to inspire people to realize they are enough.

I want to leave behind evidence of whatever tools I find that made things easier for me so others might apply them to their own lives should they deem them useful.

I want to be fit well into my old age because you have nothing if you don't have your health but also because I'm vain.

I want to die peacefully, without fear, and donate all my organs so my heart can continue to beat well after I die and so another can see through my eyes all the beautiful things I have seen.

Thank You For Seeing Her

I recently went to visit a friend at the hospital. Her three-year-old daughter was diagnosed with leukemia.

I saw an army of people coming in and out of her room: doctors and nurses, all efficient and focused, but also taking the time to show both empathy and compassion.

It was an admirable display of humanness.

On my way out, inside the very crowded elevator was a woman slumped in a wheelchair. She looked gaunt, gray, hairless, hopeless. A man stood behind her holding the handles of the wheelchair. He too looked wiped out.

Cancer took my Dad's life a year ago so I stood in that elevator feeling quite overwhelmed.

I took a step towards this woman, this stranger, and grabbed her hand. She looked up at me surprised and gripped my fingers tightly.

We stepped out of the elevator and I gave her a parting hug, then walked down the hall to the door.

"Wait!" The man who had been standing behind her caught up to me.

"I want to thank you for what you did," he said. "Ever since my wife got sick people look away. Thank you for seeing her. Thank you for holding her hand."

"No," I said. "She was holding mine."

I Want Weed

I'm standing at the front of the line to have dinner at El Techo in The Mission.

A woman comes up behind me.

"Whoa," she says. *"How long have you been waiting?"*

Me: *"A couple of minutes."*

Her: *"What's it like inside?"*

Me: *"It's a rooftop. The view is incredible."*

Her: *"Look. I just want some weed."*

Me: *"Well, the food is good."*

Her: *"Dude. I. Just. Want. Weed."*

Me: *"I'm sorry I can't help you."*

Her: *"I don't understand! Why are you here? What's going on? Where's the weed?"*

It's not until later, when I come out of the restaurant, that I notice the neighboring building is a medical pot dispensary.

This Is Crap

One of the reasons I'm taking a break from work is to write this book I've been arduously working on.

The past few weeks I've felt the whole thing is worthless crap that must be thrown out.

Except it dawned on me that anyone who has written a book has felt this way.

Ergo, everything is right where it should be.

Sigh.

Freedom

Age set me free in a way that cracked open my once puny notion of freedom.

As I have gotten older I have become more of a spectator and less of a participant. I participate just as much as I used to but I somehow witness everything too and it delights me.

I am in less of a hurry. I derive a lot of joy in watching things unfold rather than attempting to manipulate the outcome.

I see now that everything is up to me and that nothing is personal.

I am less goal-oriented and partake in things for their own sake and for the pleasure they bring me.

I radically believe in miracles because I see them everywhere.

I have absolutely lost interest in getting people to see things my way.

I have learned that all those times I thought I had to choose the choice was only in my mind because in real life there are no dichotomies.

I am beginning to doubt that the things I used to fear actually exist.

Death is not what we think it is, all darkness.

I am happy in ways I would have neither predicted nor understood even ten years ago.

Your Seat Cushion Is A Flotation Device

On days when I feel alone I pay special attention to all the things that make us feel supported, like safety nets for acrobats, harnesses for rock climbers, and subjects for kings.

Sailors have knots and sails and yogis have the floor.

In Savasana it's the Earth that holds us and it occurs to me it's always there beyond the yoga studio.

I have a forest green painting in my bedroom of an apple looking at its own reflection titled "What loneliness?"

My mom gave it to me in my early teens to remind me that no matter what I'd always have myself.

I begin to notice mirrors in improbable public places and wink at her sometimes.

This is what I'm thinking as I walk down the airplane aisle looking for my seat and find it and settle in and notice the label right before my eyes.

Your seat cushion is a flotation device.

The world is replete with flotation devices ready for you.

Keep an eye out and you will see them everywhere.

A Keeper

When the gentleman currently known as Boyfriend and I were just beginning to date, we stopped at a gas station.

There was a homeless guy there. He shuffled over, slurring and rambling incoherently.

He looked Boyfriend over and turned to me.

"Hey," he said. *"This one's a keeper."*

Are We There Yet?

There were moments in my childhood where I had it pretty rough. For example, my father used to make me wait at least an hour between eating a meal and being allowed back in the swimming pool.

This might sound like a reasonable request to you. You are obviously severely underestimating the fact that an hour to a seven-year-old girl — particularly one who loves being in the water — is like forever.

I would excuse myself from the table, brush my teeth, change my T-shirt, pace around, read a book, pretend to play chess, throw myself on the bed and count the bricks in the ceiling over my head.

How much longer now?

51 minutes.

Flash forward seven years. Chemistry class. 45 minutes of pure, hallucination-inducing torture. I would stare at the clock over the blackboard. Draw my name in bold letters on the sides of my sneakers. Scribble a note and pass it to someone. Anyone? Raise my hand and ask permission to go to the bathroom. Saunter along the school hall, *a paso de gallo — gallina* (where you put the heel of your left foot right up against the toe of your right foot, then switch feet). Arrive at the lavatory. Rinse my face. Squash my nose against the mirror to see how I would look up really close. Find gum in my back pocket. Unwrap it. Put it in my mouth. Chew. Return to class.

38 minutes to go.

Now, I can't seem to stop it. We have lunch with friends and calculate, incredulously, how long it's been since we last saw each other. We promise our families we won't let too much time go by without seeing them, and before we turn our backs on them at the airport, it's been more than a year since our last trip. Early February, I was talking to a friend and asked how her baby was doing (feeling pretty proud I remembered she'd had one). *"Dushka,"* she said, *"he's nine."*

Who came up with this thing we call time? Do we travel through it, or vice versa? Who determines how fast or how slow it should go? Is it constant, or does it play tricks on us? Does it vary per individual? Does it exist at all?

I'm looking at a photo my Mom took of me. I must have been around six.

My mother swears she took it only yesterday.

In My Life

My best friend lives in Costa Rica. Aside from living in different countries we have very different lives. Sometimes I don't see her (or talk to her) for years at a time.

The last reunion was accidental. We had a coincidental three hour layover in the Mexico City airport. We caught up on our lives and it felt like we had never spent time apart.

The fact we seldom see each other is irrelevant to me. She is, in every way that counts, "in my life".

Life is better when we broaden our parameters to make room for important people.

The whims of life don't set the rules. Circumstances don't set the rules.

The content of my heart sets the rules.

Nine Blankets

I came to visit my Mom for a few days and stayed in the room I used to sleep in when I was little.

I went to bed and was surprised at how heavy the blankets felt on me.

I turned the light back on and counted them.

Nine. She put nine blankets on my bed to make sure I wouldn't be cold.

I love you too, Mom.

Mad Crush

I have a mad crush on the poet Rumi.

Whenever I read something he wrote I wonder who on Earth could possibly think like that.

Some of the things he says get me thinking for days.

"What you seek is seeking you."

Or

"Yesterday I was clever, so I wanted to change the world.

Today I am wise, so I am changing myself."

I find others incredibly romantic.

"Out beyond ideas of wrongdoing and rightdoing there is a field.

I will meet you there."

Or

"I closed my mouth and spoke to you in a hundred silent ways."

Other quotes hit me like an arrow to my heart, like this one, which he wrote about worry:

"Why do you stay in prison when the door is so wide open?"

Some deeply inspire me.

"Stop acting so small. You are the universe in ecstatic motion."

Or this beautiful one:

"Set your life on fire. Seek those who fan the flames."

He has gotten me through grief.

"The cure of pain is in the pain."

Or

"Darkness is your candle."

He has gotten me through heartbreak.

"You have to keep breaking your heart until it opens."

And some of the things he said are so beautiful and ring so true to me that I just wish I could have met him.

Be stunned, as I was, by this quote:

"You are not a drop in the ocean. You are the entire ocean in a drop."

Sigh.

Don't Call Me

Please don't call me.

I'm an introvert. When I hear the phone ring I feel at best interrupted, at worst invaded.

This feeling is prevalent even when I'm really happy to hear from the person whose name is on my screen.

Terrible Student

I couldn't put it off any longer.

The day had come where my Dad was going to have to sign my report card.

I had no idea how I would survive this. I mean, I had flunked every possible subject.

Him: *"Oh my god. You flunked every possible subject."*

Me: —

Him: *"How do you flunk drawing?"*

Me: —

Him: *"How do you flunk SPORTS?"*

Me: —

Him: *"You're grounded. You're not leaving your room. You're not using the phone."*

Me: —

This unfortunate incident happened when I was thirteen.

A couple of years later I went into my father's library and noticed on his desk a few old photographs and some small notebooks.

The notebooks were his report cards.

I looked through them. Whoa. He had been a terrible student. There was one year in particular where he flunked every possible subject. Even drawing. Even sports.

Parents don't tell you this, but they are so much more like you than you could ever imagine.

Things I'm Afraid Of

I am afraid of my intentions being misunderstood.

Of the inevitable distance between me and those I love who I seldom see.

Of letting an important friendship go stale and sit at the bottom of a chipped white cup.

I am not afraid of losing someone over everything but I am afraid of losing someone over nothing.

I am afraid of carelessness because it implies hurting someone without even knowing.

I am so sorry.

I am afraid of being lied to.

I am afraid of the worst in me ever winning over the best of me.

I am afraid of anything happening to anyone I love.

Please no they are so beautiful

I am afraid of being a victim of violent crime. I have had a gun to my head and live with the damage it inflicted on my sense of order.

I am afraid of being a burden. I am afraid of losing my mind. I saw my Dad lose his and it was merciless.

I am afraid of having an answer to an important question no one ever thinks to ask.

Get Out

I have been married twice.

The first time I got married I was in my early twenties.

I returned from the honeymoon and regarded my life: a stunningly handsome husband and a beautiful house with French doors that opened up to a sunny patio.

I knew in my bones everything was wrong.

This feeling was hard to reconcile. I had everything I wanted.

It was hard to reconcile because aside from having everything I wanted there was absolutely nothing wrong with my new husband. He was a perfectly nice guy that would be perfect for a lucky girl somewhere.

Just not for me.

I could not rationally explain what I knew in my heart to be true: this was not going to work and I needed to get out.

Get out get out get out.

I told my parents I wanted to leave my new husband and they were shocked. They both shook their heads. My friends were shocked. They shook their heads.

It's not that I didn't care what anyone said. It's that what I said was so much louder.

I left. Against what everyone advised I left, and soon after got a divorce.

My marriage lasted less than 8 months.

Everyone told me leaving would be a mistake, that it would *"ruin my life"*. The way I saw it, the marriage was the mistake and the divorce was the solution, and the quicker I got out the less of a mess I would make of my life.

It was staying that would ruin my life: the result of "sticking with it" would mean precious time and maybe children that would tie me to this man forever.

This was over 20 years ago and I still cannot believe I had the presence of mind to leave.

I will always support what my gut tells me, even if I'm the only one who hears it, even if I cannot articulate it well enough for it to "make sense".

I will always listen to myself and as such I will never be alone.

Weekend Plans

Barista: *"Do you have any awesome plans for the weekend?"*

Me: *"WHOA YES I SURE DO."*

Barista: *"What will you be doing?"*

Me: *"Nothing."*

My Spirit Animal

I am naturally exuberant. A doctor warned me once that I was afflicted by "excessive enthusiasm".

I had to agree.

I find everything amazing and am easily impressed, amused, entertained or in awe.

Among people I know and love I'm a hugger; unless Boyfriend is coming home in which case I'm more of a respectful, gentle pouncer.

Despite aspiring to loiter I'm afraid that most frequently I bound rather than saunter.

I love naps and soft things and stare adoringly into the eyes of anyone who is kind enough to make me food.

I don't like crowds or loud noises and am easily spooked. My idea of a perfect evening involves quiet, something good to eat and snuggling.

Boyfriend smells delicious. I often very discreetly lean in to give him a loving kiss and, imperceptible to the naked eye, I close my eyes and sniff him.

Him: *"Oh my god did you just sniff me?"*

Me: *"That's preposterous. Of course not."*

I am loyal and protective (despite being clear on the fact that, alas, nobody I know needs me to protect them) and somewhat territorial: I like my space just so.

Early on, as Boyfriend was getting to know me he began referring to me as "puppy" as a term of endearment.

When my close friends heard this (*"Hey, Puppy? Can you pass the salt?"*) their reaction, rather than the bewilderment I expected was more like *"OH MY GOD THAT IS SO PERFECT SHE IS TOTALLY A PUPPY WHOA!"*

So, yeah. A happy, shaggy (not shorn or coiffed), standard poodle is my spirit animal.

Gross

When my brother was little he was in a hotel swimming pool, sneezed, saw his bugger floating in the water and was so grossed out by it he threw up.

After that we had the pool all to ourselves.

How To Date An Introvert

A couple of weeks ago I got the flu. I didn't take care of myself very well. I had to take four 5 hour flights over the course of a few days and I probably should have cancelled them and stayed home.

I ended up with acute bronchitis, which required antibiotics and bed rest.

During this same time frame, Boyfriend was dealing with massive amounts of work.

As a result of this combination of events I was home alone all day with zero social interaction for nearly two weeks.

One evening Boyfriend arrived at a reasonable hour and specifically asked if I was "starved for company".

Huh?

"I feel terrible I've barely been around! You must be dying to talk to someone!"

I had no idea what he was referring to.

I read, I wrote, I hung out, I contemplated new ways to organize my closet.

To me, the two weeks were bliss.

Dating an introvert means understanding that the person you share your life with sometimes needs to be alone and that it has nothing to do with you. It means you are free to pursue your own requirements and your own interests.

You don't have to concern yourself with your introverts. Just love them. Love them madly.

Let It Heal You

"There is nothing to writing," Hemingway said. *"All you do is sit down at the typewriter and bleed."*

I don't know why we find the notion that something tortures us alluring.

"Find what you love," said Bukowski *"and let it kill you."*

There's no denying it. It's a stunning quote.

Except, it's not necessarily true.

I love writing so much I feel I have to stand up for it.

At the risk of sounding anticlimactic, I'd rather find what I love and realize that I've found something to live for.

At the risk of sounding totally uncool, writing brings me nothing but pleasure. I am happiest when I'm at my computer.

Writing doesn't make me bleed.

It heals me.

Drunken Sailor

I am extremely neat (to a fault). Boyfriend tends more towards chaos. While we don't fight about our differences, the fact that he leaves things in nonsensical places and that I *"move his stuff"* (also known as putting it away) creates a certain comical tension.

Despite this marked contrast, Boyfriend surprised me some time ago by declaring that I *"load the dishwasher like a drunken sailor."*

Every other day or so I open the dishwasher to find bowls and dishes lined in tight, gorgeous, symmetrical rows of what I can only describe as mathematical precision.

Opening the dishwasher delights me.

Please Forgive Me

I am peppy and energetic and social and have a tendency to talk to strangers.

I find people incredibly interesting and can be extremely chatty.

I speak my mind and am not shy — not even a tiny little bit.

Given all of this, I can't blame fellow humans for mistaking me for an extrovert.

The truth is I recharge by being alone.

I need to be alone a lot. Left to my own devices I'd seldom go out.

I detest parties and cannot stand small talk.

I never pick up my phone.

If I am feeling depleted I have trouble mustering the energy to even say hello.

I have been known to miss parties of people I love, and sometimes, when I need to leave, will cut people off mid-sentence, become short, curt, rude.

Boyfriend knows that *"it's time to go"* is a code red.

He often sees the transformation from social to *"I need to leave"* and says that it's like living with someone with an "on/off" switch.

That's definitely how it feels.

This is one of my biggest battles. Figuring out how to balance my hunger for space and silence with my love for my friends (and people in general).

If I walk away from you, leave early or cut a conversation short please forgive me.

I just want to go home.

Soup

I am making soup.

My first step is to chop up a huge pile of vegetables.

Before I consider this soup "ready" I will strain it. There will be no trace of some of the things I used to make it delicious, such as the papery skin of an onion, the brown ends of a carrot, the tough, fibrous broccoli stems.

But all of these things will contribute to the flavor of the final soup.

One hundred years from now there will be no trace of me.

But I believe that with my actions, however small, I leave something behind that contributes to the taste of what I'll call the final cosmic soup.

And this is why everything I do matters.

Artificial Intelligence

"Both you and your baby are free to go home," the doctor told my Mom.

They had spent two days in the emergency room at the hospital because my brother was having trouble breathing.

"You can go home now" was all my mother wanted to hear. It sounded like all her wishes had been granted.

She wrapped up my brother in a blanket and strode out. Then she stopped at the frame of the hospital door, turned around and went back inside.

"Something is wrong," she told the doctor. *"I know the tests don't show anything but something is wrong."*

My Mom was right. My brother would have died of acute respiratory distress if she had not turned around, if she had not pushed back on the very declaration that confirmed everything she wanted, if she had been afraid of the doctor thinking she was being "difficult".

Instinct. Computers will never have the instinct to override instructions.

Lethal Aim

I never fit in.

I was awkward. I never knew what the right thing to say was (Believe me, I tried.). I didn't understand what to wear or how. I was the last to be picked in gym class. I was seldom invited to parties.

When I was, I stood in a corner wishing, as we say in Mexico, that the ground would swallow me.

The popular kids always hung out together, a continuous, rowdy gathering; a pack with shiny, sleek hair, musky perfume and the right jeans. They sat at the back of the class. They laughed and jostled and pranked each other.

They were so beautiful.

There was one girl, blue-eyed, freckled, sandy, lanky, who always made fun of me. She was a bully. She wasn't violent or aggressive but she was cruel. I was afraid of her.

In my memory, school was hard. I couldn't find my place. I skipped class and slinked around, wishing I could be invisible.

One day not too long ago this same girl sent me a Facebook invite with a note. I am from Mexico so it was in Spanish.

It went something like this:

"Dushka, I haven't seen you in over thirty years. I think of you often, your wit and how comfortable you were with yourself. It was like you were above the effort I had to make to remain popular. I struggled to fit in. I wished I was more like you."

Huh?

A part of me wanted to point out how mean she had been (to me and others), the knack she had to make me feel small; that impeccable, lethal aim.

But I couldn't bring myself to. Instead I accepted her friend request and occasionally see her on my feed.

We all harbor feelings of inadequacy and isolation. How real are they? How many people that look good from where we stand are in the grip of these same feelings?

It's our insecurities that possess that impeccable, lethal aim. They play tricks on us.

It turns out that we are all more alike than we are different.

My Parents' Weddings

I attended my Mom's wedding to the man she married after my father and her split up. By then, they had been together for about ten years. I was fifteen.

The wedding was at our house. My Mom was nervous and tipsy (she doesn't typically drink very much, but she was drinking on that day). She was acting erratic and he was looking at her adoringly. I stood next to them while they said their vows.

Afterwards someone asked me what it felt like to "finally" be a family. I replied we had been one all along.

I also attended my Dad's wedding to his third wife (when he married his second wife, the woman he married after my Mom, I was too little. Otherwise I'm sure I would have gone to that wedding too).

They got married on the beach. She wore bright red, and the dress had a short skirt that looked like a glittering tutu.

They both looked radiant and giddy, like they were getting away with something insane and delightful.

What I felt at the time is the same thing I feel now.

All we want for the people that we love is that they be loved. That they be looked at adoringly. That the people they choose to be with feel like they are getting away with something insane and delightful.

And thank you. Thank you so much for loving my parents.

I Get Away With Nothing

The last time Boyfriend was away on a trip I decided I'd wear his cozy robe.

It's soft, it's plushy, it's deliciously big on me.

I'd use it in his absence, then throw it in the wash. He'd never know.

Cocooned and comfy I set out to make myself a cup of tea.

That's when the dangling sleeve of the robe caught fire.

I waved my arm around in a panic before recalling I needed to tuck and roll.

I was reminded of so many things I thought I already knew.

Secrets, no matter how big or how insignificant, are not worth keeping.

When it comes to sneakiness and stealth, I can get away with nothing.

You can't wash out a burn on plushy, cozy fabric.

Most importantly, I really do need to stay out of the kitchen.

Perfectly Symmetrical

I bound out of bed before 6:30 a.m.

Just the thought of sleeping in makes me feel restless.

I stand on my head every day. I don't need a wall for support, unless it's a handstand, which I also do every day.

I like being upside down.

I climb trees. I have hideouts.

Sometimes I read under the sheets with a flashlight.

Sometimes I lie there and count the wooden beams over my head.

I feel awe and enthusiasm regularly, regard most things with wonder, am madly impatient and am ashamed to admit I experience the occasional temper tantrum.

Are we there yet?

I believe in the people that I love, ignore my limits, arrange my clothes by color, line up my shoes, sustain that life is simple, clap when I'm pleased and find a lot of things funny.

I really would rather be an amateur.

I sing loudly to every song I know the lyrics of and play it over and over even after someone begs for mercy. Just one more, I promise.

I don't mind making a fool of myself and most of the time resist eating dessert first but always want to.

I am very, very responsible and yet think back on the days when I used to have adult supervision. It's not that I miss them, but I deeply appreciate that I had them.

I didn't know. I didn't know that when you took care of me you were just a kid.

I have for some time now been tying my own shoelaces. They look perfectly symmetrical.

Powerful Sorceress

When I'm about to cross the street and there is a "Don't Walk" sign, I wave my hand at it like a nonchalant, powerful sorceress to turn it to green.

Once I was standing next to a woman and her kid. He was around six. My wave of the hand was perfectly timed and the light turned green right when it needed to. The kid's jaw dropped to the floor.

I winked at him, blew on my fingers and crossed the street, coat flapping in the wind.

I secretly believe it was less a matter of timing and more a matter of magic.

Mother Bear

I went to elementary school in Mexico City.

I was in English class, taking a test.

This class was a breeze for me because my mother was born in the United States and spoke English to me from birth.

I was abysmal at other things, but not at this.

A classmate raised his hand.

"No me siento bien, maestra," he said. *"Me arde mucho la garganta."*

"This is English class," she replied. *"You cannot be excused until you say it in English."*

He looks at her.

"Repeat after me," she says. *"I don't feel well. I have a throat ache."*

He looks at her.

"He doesn't have throat ache," I say. *"What he has is a sore throat."*

The teacher glares at me. *"Throat ache, Dushka. Repeat it after me."*

"But, it's wrong."

"I will deduct a point from the exam you are about to turn in," she says. *"Make a note of why: Throat. Ache."*

That evening my Mom asks about my day and I recount what happened. It was not my intent to tell on the teacher. Rather, the incident had frustrated me and I wanted to share my disbelief.

My mother is a woman full of power and magic.

I see her unfurl before my eyes: loving — interested — inquisitive — alert — indignant — ferocious — Mother Bear — incensed.

"She made you repeat this?" she asks.

"Yes."

"She deducted a point off your exam?"

"Yes."

She takes me to school herself the next day. I don't know exactly what happens but my exam is returned to me with a large A scribbled on top a few days later.

The grade was fair. Most notably, no points were deducted.

All these years later, my Mom still sometimes mutters, *"Throat ache. Throat ache! Humph."*

Things I Like

I like spending time under water, the buoyancy and broken light.

Arranging things in rows.

I enjoy cleaning out my closet more than I like shopping.

I like eating broccoli more than eating bacon.

I enjoy talking to strangers and leaving early.

I like considering that writing can be thermodynamic: arranging words to maybe generate a spark. Not on the page. In you.

I like celebrating things no one has an anniversary for. Remember the very first time we ever took a flight together?

I like pencils. My planner is a paper notebook.

I like waking up before anyone else.

I like being the one who loves more.

In My Thirties

Me: *"Dad, I am leaving tomorrow morning for a business trip."*

Dad: *"Who is going with you?"*

Me: *"Uh, nobody."*

Dad: *"Then how will you get there?"*

Me: *"I will board a plane."*

Dad: *"Alone?"*

Me: *"Well, with other passengers."*

Dad: *"Call me the moment you land."*

To our parents, we never stop being little kids.

Chatter Brain

I have a monkey brain.

I am in the midst of loud, demanding, constant chatter who sees metaphors for life everywhere, wants to write everything down and obsesses about what I need to do next and how I'm going to get there.

Sitting cross-legged in absolute silence and just paying attention to my breath is really, really hard; some days impossible.

I just want to go over my schedule one more time.

This is why I respond well to guided meditation, a soft, gentle, firm voice that reminds me to *let my thoughts pass like leaves floating in a river.*

Sit down. Let the dust settle. Focus on your breath. Be fascinated by its texture.

Whenever your thoughts distract you — and they will always distract you — just come back to your breath. There is nothing you need to do right now. Nowhere you need to be. Just for now, return to your breath.

Through the whole process I am convinced that I'm "doing it wrong" and feel twitchy and like I want to run but afterwards I feel such clarity and peace.

Ugly But Good

One of my favorite pastries are Brutti ma Buoni *(ugly yet good).*

They are amorphous blobs of heaven, made from egg whites, hazelnuts and sugar (no flour, no butter).

Some time ago while traveling through Italy I was determined to find the best ones, which would require sampling one at each *pasticceria.*

Despite the simple ingredients, the flavor and consistency vary greatly, from airy to crunchy to chewy to everything in between.

It was in Cogne, a jewel of a town deep in a narrow valley, that I encountered the roundest, puffiest, most harmonious looking *brutti ma buoni.*

I walked in and aghast, told the owner *"These cannot possibly be considered brutti ma buoni. They aren't at all ugly."*

"Regretfully, signora, we make everything in our pastry shop beautiful. These are indeed brutti ma buoni, only they are not brute."

I looked around. This was truly a gorgeous pastry shop. Cookies piled high with different flavors of jam, goodies swirled in chocolate, meringues coiffed in cream, almond paste filled croissants dusted in confectioner's sugar.

At the time, I granted them the award for the best.

I will have to go again and embark on a similar search. It's been a few years, and there is only one way to know for sure that their recipe has remained consistent.

Not Meant For Forever

I used to believe that a relationship that ended in a break-up was one that had failed.

But I have had many that revealed to me another way of looking at the world, contributed to my growth, changed me.

Some altered the course of my life.

They are a part of my history and the person I have become.

I have learned relationships are not necessarily meant to last forever, and that it's possible to have a successful one that runs its course and leaves behind two people who are better for having been a part of it.

"Forever" is not a measure for success.

Boyfriend Bait

The biggest lie I ever told Boyfriend was a lie of omission.

We were moving in together and our new place was filled with boxes. We were ferociously unpacking. I am single-minded, and all I could think of was *"I will finish before I go back to work on Monday."*

All I could think of was that I would stop at nothing until everything was in its place.

Or so he thought.

I sat on one of the boxes, trying to look like I'd had it.

Me: *"Can we please take an hour and go out to get a quick bite? I need a mental break."*

Him: *"Whah?"*

Me: *"I feel that if I just take a bit of time I will come back with renewed focus."*

Him: *"Whah?"*

Me: *"Come on. Pick a place. Don't tell me you're not hungry."*

Him: *"What about sushi?"*

Me: *"What about the bar you like? You can get a Manhattan and we'll come right back."*

Him: *"OK!"*

When we arrived at the bar, 40 of his friends were already there, ready to celebrate his birthday.

Manhattans: Boyfriend bait.

How We Think

One of my oldest friends (we met when I was three and he was five) is a musician.

Over the last four decades we see each other sporadically rather than regularly but it's like he has a window into my spirit. Even after many years of not seeing each other we pick up where we left off.

For us, "catching up" means I go to his house, sit in his music room and listen to his latest work. While I listen, he pores through everything I've written.

"How?" I asked him once. (He must have been around 19.) *"How can you compose music? I don't understand!"*

"Dushka," he said to me. *"I think in notes. You think in words."*

New Word Needed

In Spanish there is a distinction between "amar" and "querer".

In English they both translate as "to love".

But how can I use the same word to tell you how I feel about my man and to explain my opinion about popcorn?

Things I Have Never Done

I have never felt unfortunate.

I have never felt unloved.

I have never packed a suitcase I couldn't carry myself.

I have never tried to fix a broken cup.

I have never crawled into bed fully dressed.

I have never held ill will for very long.

I have never felt incapable of improvising, which is all anybody ever does.

I have never learned from the first mistake or even the second.

Alas, I have never managed to be in two places at once.

I have never understood why he had to die the way he did.

I don't think I ever will.

Born Again

My parents divorced when I was three years old.

They both had incredibly strong personalities and madly pursued their passions, interests and path.

I learned by example that one must strive to be happy.

Their relationship was contentious, despite of which they never spoke ill of each other.

They were very, very different people but were in lockstep regarding how to raise us.

It was less about eating our vegetables and more about making sure we trusted our own gut and thought for ourselves.

They trusted me to make my own decisions. They had strict rules and boundaries when it came to my safety (such as getting home at a reasonable hour) but were completely hands-off when it came to my choices (they insisted on meeting my friends but never, ever approved or disapproved of anyone I brought home).

They specifically, deliberately raised me religionless.

They exposed me to as much culture as they could. Every room in the house had a bookshelf, both houses a library. I was not allowed to watch cartoons or Walt Disney movies and was taken to every possible museum and archeological site. We traveled as much as we could. I was raised bilingual (when I learned to talk I did so in both English and Spanish).

They loved me ferociously, sometimes with exasperation, sometimes with perplexity, but most often with delight.

I would be born to them again if I could.

What If Your Boyfriend Cheated On You?

When I think about Boyfriend the first word that comes to mind is "solid". He's a solid character, a good man, and him cheating on me would surprise me.

As such, even before feeling what you would expect, I would be concerned about him. He would be acting out of character so I would want to make sure he was OK.

I would then take my anger and grief and deal with these two companions alone. Screaming bloody murder and threatening homicide are not as satisfying (to me) as one would expect. I would instead want to handle things with grace. It has the best aftertaste and feeling proud of how I dealt with things would aid in the subsequent mending of my heart.

Finally, I'd want us to be friends. We have built a lot together and I'd want to salvage rather than destroy. I would prefer not to discard people who are important to me.

I'd also ask him to teach me how to use an espresso machine.

I'd never want anyone else to make me coffee.

Unknown Universe

There was this couple sitting across from me on the bus.

I strained to eavesdrop.

They whispered. They giggled. They pouted. They laughed. They nuzzled. They leaned into each other. They held hands.

It was a rough commute: a whole universe unfolding before me, and I couldn't hear a thing.

Broken Glass

I was in a car crash in my early twenties. On impact I felt a gripping pain in my lower back. I immediately checked if I could move my toes, my legs. I was terrified something had happened to my spinal cord.

I turned to look at my friend, who was driving. There was blood everywhere. She had one hand resting on my shoulder. Another on the steering wheel. Another on her lap.

Wait a minute.

The hand on my shoulder was my own.

The impossible angle my hand was in was later explained by the fact my humerus was shattered. The X-ray didn't look like a fracture. It looked like broken glass.

My arm didn't hurt until later. It took several hours for the adrenaline of the accident to wear off. I went into surgery quickly and was in a cast for 10 months.

Before this incident I was afflicted by an illusion of invincibility. This was my first real encounter with my own mortality.

In the following months the pain in my arm was terrible, sharp and always startling, but what was worse was feeling helpless. In the days after the first surgery I needed assistance to shower, to get dressed, lace my shoes.

I was in college and working as a columnist for a newspaper and writing without my right hand was pure, undiluted frustration. My body couldn't keep up with what my brain was trying to dictate.

I couldn't write.

Soon, anything I tried to do seemed too difficult. I found it increasingly hard to get out of bed.

What I would want someone with a broken bone to know is that an accident that results in this kind of injury also dislodges something inside you.

You are hurt and your abilities are limited and you have to respect the fact that you need time to adjust, to mend.

Slow down. Be patient with yourself. Give yourself that.

A File Marked "Dushka"

I am in Mexico visiting my Mom.

My Dad died over a year ago and I spent some time going over the last bit of his files.

He was organized and threw out as much as he could so he wouldn't have to put it away.

I have this clear memory of him quickly glancing at correspondence before shredding it and tossing it.

He deeply appreciated not being burdened by too much paper.

I discovered today he kept everything I ever gave him: every sketch, every drawing, every letter.

He's been gone for over a year and still finds a way to tell me he loves me.

Give Me Space

You're listening to the radio and turn the dial and it goes from a clear stream of words or music to loud, deafening static.

LOUD DEAFENING STATIC THAT HURTS YOUR EARS AND FILLS YOUR HEAD.

So now you don't want music. You just need to turn the darn thing off.

This is how I perceive the world. Streams of words or music that suddenly become unintelligible.

It all becomes too much.

It'smyphonemessagesandsocialmediabutnotjusthatitsthepeople Ineedtotalktoit'sbeenmonthssincellastsawyouwhenwhencanwe gettogetherthereisapartyI'mthrowingapartyyoucantmissityoum issedthelastonewehavetogowecan'tnotgobutiwanttowriteplease justgivemeabitofspaceIneedspacePLEASE STOP.

Please stop.

I close the door and turn my phone off and take a shower and sit on a comfortable chair and just...sit.

Sometimes an evening is enough but sometimes I need to not be around so many people and so much noise for a while.

I'd like to step into another dimension so I can move through the world and witness all this beauty unperturbed but I can't so my only recourse is to take a break.

My need to take a break has nothing to do with my love or appreciation or gratitude to the people I shut out.

It's just something I need to give myself, and as much as I love others, I can't live without it.

To The Other Women

When I met Boyfriend he was in his forties. He arrived with a past, including a failed marriage. This man knew what he wanted, knew himself and his patterns, and clearly recognized when we fought or disagreed where the line was between my work and his.

He didn't materialize into existence like this.

I like to think that I have suffered and been (unintentionally) hurt by men who were made better by what they learned with me, and then proceeded to lovingly deliver them — improved — into someone else's arms.

This is why I received Boyfriend in his current glorious state.

To all the women who have been in the lives of the men I have loved, thank you.

And, you're welcome.

Not My Calling

I took a self-defense class once.

The guy who taught it explained how to position my fingers so I could gouge out the eyes of my hypothetical attacker.

I looked at him.

He asked if I had any questions.

"But, what if I hurt him?"

I am ill-suited to be a supervillian.

I Believe

I believe I write my own book of fate and that no story I ever come up with is either indelible nor immutable.

I believe we are all eternal and that death is not what we think.

I believe there is no design in either accidents nor coincidences.

I believe in colossal good fortune.

I have won every lottery.

I believe everyone who appears in my life to love, help or hurt me does so as a teacher because this notion is conducive to gratitude and gratitude is the closest I have ever come to feeling the presence of God.

Thank you. Thank you for your lies. Thank you for your textures, the velvet earlobes and scratchy beard and faint spirals on the pads of your fingers.

Thank you for letting me press up my ear against yours so I could hear the ocean.

Thank you for sleeping while I read my future in the palms of your hands.

Of course I believe in "the one". Except, I get many. And I don't walk the world wondering where they are.

I instead conjure them as I tame the monsters that exist within me.

Why Do We Want To Protect Those We Love?

I have a friend who is all effort and discipline and grit.

She does things in earnest and with her whole heart and I dig that.

She was recently telling me about something someone said that hurt her.

I caught a quick glimpse of disarray in that compact, resolute spirit. Fleeting, reversible, inconsequential; yet piercing and vulnerable.

We are all fragile, aren't we?

We want to protect the people that we love because buried deep into our composition we carry a primal command to guard what is beautiful.

Methodical

Boyfriend stands in the middle of the kitchen, his fancy Japanese knife in one hand, his knife sharpener in the other.

Whoosh. Whoosh. Whoosh. Whoosh.

He sharpens the knife before he uses it, every time, no exceptions.

He is lackadaisical and laid back and messy so I find his methodical knife rituals incongruous and insanely attractive.

If I lovingly take a knife and gently attempt to slice an apple on the counter *"DUSHKA NO USE A BOARD YOU CAN'T CUT DIRECTLY ON THE COUNTER ACK HERE I WILL DO IT!"*

I am discouraged from approaching the knives. I am deterred from loading the dishwasher.

I am forbidden to soak and properly clean his very oily cast iron pans.

I am excited to report the kitchen is becoming off limits.

Not Far From The Tree

My parents tried for a long time to have a baby and could not get pregnant.

Legend has it they tried to conceive for seven years.

And one day, there I was.

My Dad used to put his hands on my mother's belly as it grew; and kiss it and hug it and jokingly say *"This one is mine. You can have the next one."*

From the second I was born people around me exclaimed I looked just like my father.

Everything I have told you up until now is the story as my mother tells it.

Despite their epic disagreements, my mother's and father's accounts regarding my creation and arrival were perfectly consistent through decades.

My own experience confirmed that *"this one"* (me) was indeed his.

When my Dad introduced me to anyone, the conversation went something like this:

My Dad: *"Aaaaand, this is Dushka."*

Visitor: "*Oh my god! No! This is uncanny! This is too much! This is not possible! She's your spitting image! Two peas in a pod! A chip off the old block! The apple doesn't fall far from the tree! Qué barbaridad! Esta niña no niega la cruz de su parroquia!*"

My Dad: "*Dushka. Say thank you.*"

Me: "*Thank you!*"

My favorite part is that being told I looked just like him made him *beam*. I felt like I belonged. Like I was loved.

It never got old.

Sometimes, my Mom would introduce me to a friend of hers who had never met my Dad. This friend would say "*Oh! She looks just like you!*" to which my Mom would reply "*that's because you haven't seen her father.*" My Mom and I would then look at each other like "*Let's cut her some slack. She just doesn't know.*"

The truth is that I can see my mother in myself. My hands are her hands. Hers are bigger, stronger, but I can see how mine were made using hers as the original model. I see her in other places too — in my back and shoulders, in my hunger and my lust for life.

Boyfriend and I have been dating for almost five years. He is relatively new in my life. He has met both my parents.

At least once a week I will do something and he will shake his head and say "*Oh my god! No! This is uncanny! This is too much! This is not possible! She's your spitting image! Two peas in a pod! A chip off the old block! The apple doesn't fall far from the tree!*"

To which I reply "*But, how would you know? He died before you really got to know him!*"

"*Dushka.*" he says. "*You are exactly like your mother.*"

I feel bewildered, taken aback, enchanted, like I've been reminded of a gift I was given a long time ago but in the fog of excessive good fortune forgot to open.

Please Be Late

I am in the lobby of my new client's building waiting for my meeting to start.

I am always early because being late stresses me too much.

This lobby is like a gorgeous, spacious living room. The couch is comfortable, I was just offered and given a cup of green tea, and I am in possession of the guest wifi code.

I am sitting here alone, peacefully, quietly, with my phone and my tea and my notes app.

Please be late client please be late because I have everything I need.

My First Friend

My father's best friend had a son who was a bit older than me.

The first time we met I must have been around three, and he must have been around five.

I have known him longer than I have known my brother.

I have a vague recollection of us playing in the garden. Yellow and red and green, a swing and the smell of grass.

We traveled together too. There is a picture somewhere of us walking on the beach in Puerto Vallarta; making snow angels when his Dad invited my family to Aspen to ski.

For the first 10 years of our life we saw each other fairly regularly because of our parents.

I was goofy and he was cool. He stood up to anyone who bullied me, partly to defend me, but mostly on principle.

For maybe seven years after that we lost touch because we started hanging out less with our parents and more with our own friends.

He spent some time abroad, then returned to Mexico (where we are from) and called me. I was maybe 17.

I went over to his parent's place, where he was staying, and it felt like discovering a treasure we had hidden in that big white house so many years before.

"What did you think the first time you saw me after so many years?"

"Hair and energy," he said.

This is a perfect description.

Ever since I've known him it has felt like we had a shorthand, our private constellation, a closed-circuit communication system.

Like all my life being misunderstood and suddenly not even having to explain myself.

Through the decades that followed, this kinship has remained the same even though we have always been in and out of touch.

Whenever we catch up and I tell him what I'm up to he listens intently and nods, then brushes everything aside.

"Stop whatever you are doing and write, Dushka."

He went off to college and lived in New York for a few years. He and his girlfriend gave me a grand tour of their apartment and I knew he was in the right place because they had a partial view of the water.

When he returned to Mexico he was nursing a broken heart and I introduced him to a girl he was briefly married to.

He must have learned all the appropriate lessons because his current wife is an angel.

I left Mexico and came to live in San Francisco, where they came to visit a few times. We all went to a Prince concert together, drank coffee and sat on a bench overlooking the ocean. We ate sushi.

"Stop what you are doing and write, Dushka."

He was one of the first people to arrive at my father's funeral and neither of us needed to say a thing.

He recently had a baby, who I held for the first time when he was about three months old. He sends me pictures of him and he's growing so quickly. He looks just like his father.

Maybe some day he will be a teenager and want to get away from his parents and come and spend some time with me.

I will tell him stories.

I hope he already hangs out with his Dad's friend's daughter. Their friendship will last for the rest of their lives.

Sobremesa

You know that time you spend sitting at the dining room table talking to your friends or family long after you have finished eating?

When I was growing up, my entire family would get together on Sundays. We'd sit down to eat at around 3:00, and then stay around the table talking until it was time for dinner.

In Spanish, the act of lingering at the table after a meal is called *sobremesa.*

There is no word for it in English.

Irresistible

I can't resist solid ground

Or swimming pools.

That crystalline glint

Taking the plunge.

I can't resist rows

The illusion of order

Buying books I might not read for years.

I can't resist

Doing just one more thing before I go.

Believing in things

I know aren't true.

Writing. Please, just one more hour.

Seeing the best in people.

This has given me so much more

Than what it's taken away.

I can't resist rejoicing

My own immortality.

Not forever.

Just right now.

I can't resist talking to strangers

Vinegar chips, poems

I can't resist throwing away what I don't need

And sometimes what I need the most.

Wide skies filled with clouds.

I can't resist good luck

More than my fair share

And I know the time is now

But I can't resist planning ahead.

Sculptor's Daughter

When I was a kid I ran across the grass surrounded by life-sized figures made of bronze.

Some were women camouflaged against dark, volcanic rock walls.

Some were felines.

Warriors kept me company, as did snakes and elephants and giraffe.

My Mom is a sculptor so playing hide and seek among the things she made seemed weird to other kids but did not seem weird to me.

What Does "Overthinking" Mean?

Inside my brain there is constant discourse.

There are many noisy voices in there talking to me and sometimes it's hard to distinguish who is being driven, who is being lazy, who is trying to push me and who is trying to take care of me.

This is why I need silence. To sort out these opinions within me, give them each their rightful place so that together we can do the best we can.

Sometimes this process is near-instant and sometimes we go in circles, in particular about simple, every day things.

Get up early and write first thing it's when your head is clearest go Dushka

Get up early and do everything you need to do to clear your plate so you can think it will be so much better

Wait a minute wait a minute this is a trap if we wait until everything is done we will never finish there will always be one more thing that has to get done let's write first

But you will be distracted don't you want to write in peace?

And that is overthinking it.

How To Care For Curly Hair

I wash my hair every day.

Hair experts gasp when I say this (sacrilege!) but I can't help it.

When I shampoo I give my scalp a good massage (mmmmm) and when I condition I comb it out with a wide tooth comb.

Then I use leave in conditioner. Before applying it I mix it in my hands with a drop of pure oil. (Argan oil or coconut oil.)

I trim it every three months or so.

That's it.

With curly hair, what I don't do is extremely important: curly hair wants to do its thing and is happiest when you leave it alone.

As such, I never tell it what to do. Because, if I'm trying to make it be something it isn't, who is the one being *unmanageable* and *difficult*?

I never brush it.

I never rub it with a towel (I lovingly wrap a towel around my head instead).

I never blow dry it. Not ever. On the rare occasions that I allow someone to drag me to a snowy location I wash my hair the night before.

I never use anything hot on it (curling irons, etc.).

I never color it, highlight it, straighten it, or otherwise force it to be something it isn't.

I never rail at it in frustration.

I never tell people with gorgeous, thick, heavy, lustrous, long, straight hair that I wish my hair was more like theirs.

Stepfather

My parents separated when I was three and divorced when I was five. They both remarried pretty quickly after that.

For the first decade of my life I lived with my Mom and saw my Dad on weekends.

From Monday to Friday I was raised by my Mom and her husband, my stepfather.

My stepfather was very involved in my upbringing. He picked me up from school, nursed me when I was sick, helped me with my homework and peppered me with questions about my day, every day.

One day I told my Dad, with my heart full of love, that I was lucky to have two dads.

He was furious.

My intent *(I am so fortunate!)* and his interpretation *(my role is being usurped!)* came from different planets and as such my words were unintentionally hurtful.

I did not mean what he thought I meant.

No one could ever threaten my father's place in my life and I was so certain of this it perplexed me that he'd even consider it a possibility.

We have an infinite ability to love people and to assign each of them their own privileged, sacred, untouchable place.

Jesus

There I was in an Uber pool. I was, like my fellow riders, absorbed into my phone mostly to not disturb anyone with impolite interaction.

The driver, weaving fast in and out of traffic suddenly exclaims *"JESUS!"* and slams on the brakes.

I jump 10 feet, actually thwack my head on the car ceiling.

All good. Jesus was the name of my co-pooler and we had arrived at his destination.

Things And Puppies

Today on my walk back home from yoga I happened upon a creature of such intense beauty and cuddliness that I thought my heart would burst.

A blue-eyed puppy.

I looked at him. He looked at me.

Our eyes locked.

Clearly, he belongs with me.

Do you mind if I say hello?

Sure thing.

Can I carry him?

Of course.

I lift him. He kisses my face and snuggles into me.

He *loves* me.

I want to make a run for it.

I WILL TAKE YOU HOME PUPPY HOLD ON TIGHT

Wait.

This would make no sense.

This puppy requires a level of care I can't give him.

With my travel schedule and work and his need for attention and stability we are not compatible.

But even if we were. He already has a loving person.

A life of his own that does not involve me.

I do the only thing I can do: I put him down and say goodbye and walk home alone.

Just because we want something doesn't mean we have any right over it.

Just because we feel love towards something and are convinced it's reciprocal it doesn't mean we must own it.

This applies to things, and puppies, and people too.

He Raised Me To Survive Him

I dream of my father and his house every single night.

He roams through each room like he did when he was still here, double checking that all the doors are locked and bolted and that his family is safe inside.

Every morning I open my eyes and think it's been too long since I last spoke to him. Too many Sundays without hearing his voice.

"Hija!"

I remember, as I adjust to my waking world, that there is a terrible, impossible reason for that.

It's the only time he's ever gone anywhere without leaving a number where I could reach him in case of an emergency.

What if there is an emergency?

That's when I recall everything he ever told me. Everything he ever taught me.

He raised me to survive him and through the years carefully, deliberately left within me everything I need.

Supremely Annoying

I can be supremely annoying.

I live mostly inside my head, require a lot of time alone, am fastidiously neat, like going over plans more times than strictly necessary, and insist on being unreasonably early to any appointment.

"OH MY GOD WHAT A PAIN IN THE ASS," Boyfriend blurts out, in a loving yet exasperated tone of voice.

"I know," I reply. *"But I love you anyway."*

Something Witchy

When I was growing up the phone would ring and the only way to tell who was calling was to answer.

There was no caller ID. You could not see the name of the caller on your screen. There was no screen.

Whenever I called my Mom, instead of saying *"Hello?"* she would pick up the phone and say *"Hi Dushka! Everything OK?"*

I would always ask how the heck she knew it was me and she would claim I would suddenly start pushing on the edges of her consciousness.

Something witchy goes on with mothers everywhere.

Books And Serendipity

A few blocks from my apartment stands a simple wooden structure filled with books.

People from the neighborhood drop off reading material they don't want anymore and others pick up what they want to read.

I got up this morning and went to run a few errands. On my way, I stopped to glance at this bookstand.

A guy walked up next to me.

Him: *"What are you looking for?"*

Me: *"That's just the thing, right? I want to find what I'm not looking for."*

Him: *"In that case, may I recommend something?"*

I stand at attention.

Him: *"Read a book by Ted Conover called Rolling Nowhere. It's epic."*

Me: *"Have you read The Drifters, by James Michener?"*

Him: *"No!"*

Me: *"Get it, and that way we will both be reading travel books recommended by strangers on a sidewalk early one Sunday morning."*

His face lights up. We high-five. I walk away.

I get home a few hours later and look up the book he recommended. It has really good reviews. I download it immediately.

Blazing, fleeting serendipity. It never fails to brighten my day.

Can We Ever Be Safe?

My five year old nephew was on a scooter, my eight year old niece on a bicycle.

My brother and I were jogging along.

Obviously, it was hard to keep up.

Suddenly my niece was sprawled on the sidewalk. She had fallen off the bike and scraped her knee. My brother was patting her down and asking her to walk around so he could assess the damage.

I was standing off to the side pondering how futile it is to try to keep the people that I love safe.

I can't. Not even when I'm running right beside them.

Boyfriend rides a motorcycle. If he ever had a bad fall I wouldn't even find out until hours later.

We chop up our heart and place the fragile pieces in the pockets of the people that we love. Then off they go, unprotected, exposed.

I've considered gathering everyone up and persuading them to live snug in a comfortable, impregnable metal box.

I'd put air holes on the top.

Still, I don't think anyone would be very happy with this arrangement.

Tragically, the people that I love are so damn picky regarding their ability to roam free.

This leaves me with two options: to live knotted up in anxiety and fear that would accomplish nothing (other than my early demise), or to have faith that things might be OK.

Friends ask me if I mind that Boyfriend rides a motorcycle. I tell them the truth. I do not. If someone told me I had to stop doing yoga due to how many people get injured I wouldn't miss a single class.

Life is risk, and we have to take it.

My brother has by now determined my niece is scraped up but otherwise unscathed. He puts his big dad hands on her tiny shoulders.

"Look, sweetheart. We've talked about this. If you want to ride a bike, you're probably going to fall. And then you get back up. Do you want to get back on, or do you want to go home?"

She looks at him, wipes her snotty face with the back of her sleeve.

"I want to get back up."

And so she does.

Culture Shock

When I first arrived in the US from Mexico someone in a meeting set down a platter of Oreo chip cookies on the center of the table.

Oreo chip cookies.

In the US, people make cookies with cookies.

What Is Wonder?

Walking around the supermarket I saw a woman pushing her baby around in the back of a shopping cart.

He was so awake, back straight, eyes wide.

Suddenly he started shrieking in astonishment.

His Mom followed his line of vision and identified the object of his manic delight.

A melon.

She grabbed the melon and put it into his outstretched arms. He hugged it like it was precious. Then he tried to gnaw it.

We were born pooping, drooling, smelly, noisy bundles of wonder.

Scratchy And Glorious
(To Eddie. I Hope You're Dancing.)

Maybe it happened during recess.

Maybe it happened after school.

"Hi. I made you a mix tape."

And he would hand you a cassette.

The best ones came wrapped in a page ripped out of a notebook.

The scrawls on the crumpled, lined sheet of paper listed out the songs now in your possession and briefly explained the reasons they were selected.

"This is the one they were playing when I first saw you the one we sang in the car the one we both shrieked we liked at the same time turn up the volume this is the one that always makes you jump up and dance haha you can't dance"

I know that today you can burn someone a CD.

It's just not the same.

A cassette tape sounded scratchy and glorious. You could never rewind it to exactly where you wanted it, *"AAAH THERE STOP THERE YOU WENT TOO FAR!"*

It got worn as you listened to it over and over (like crimson and clover).

On calamitous, harrowing days the darn thing, practically your most precious possession, would get tangled in the stereo of your car.

You would need a Bic pen to lovingly, patiently scroll it back in.

I miss mix tapes and the entire weekends I spent choosing and assembling the ones I would offer as gifts.

I miss calling friends up to ask if they had the records I would need.

I miss finding the friend whose dad had the very best stereo.

The creation of a good mix tape was a work of art that took a village.

I miss the mix tapes I was given, the hidden messages I read too much into, or not enough.

I'm sorry I didn't know you were in love with me.

Mix tapes punctuated my life, each rasping song a permanent imprint of a road trip, a blue-eyed boy, a time, a sleepless night, unrequited love.

I Can't Pronounce That

I have a long list of words I mispronounce because I read them before hearing them.

The one that comes up most often is archieenemy.

I don't know how this happened.

Boyfriend: *"Archieenemy?"*

Me: *"Yeah. He's his archieenemy."*

Boyfriend: *"By which of course you mean archenemy."*

Me: *"Yeah. Archieenemy."*

Boyfriend: *"Archenemy."*

Me: *"Yeah. That."*

I Remember

My Mom and Dad installed a child-proof gate at the top of the stairs so I wouldn't fall.

I learned right away how to open it and remember my parents coming out of their bedroom in the middle of the night, alarmed, to scoop me up and gently place me back in my cradle.

The last time we all lived in the same house I was three years old.

I remember my red velvet dress; the risers of the stairs at the house I grew up in. They were a blue and white tile I could see at eye level as I crawled up.

I remember making bread with my Mom, or squishing the flour between my fingers (and toes) while my Mom made bread.

Memorizing the *"I think mice are very nice"* poem I learned in first grade. I still know it by heart.

After my parents split up, my Dad built a house where he would live for the rest of his life. I remember seeing that house for the first time, the giant white banister, the dining room table and the library where he'd spend most of Saturday afternoons.

I remember waiting for my Mom's husband to come home. He always got me something enrapturing. He is an artist, so I remember beads, shiny things, and the smell of oil paints and thinner.

Going to the toy store every Sunday with my Dad to ogle things and permission to pick one small thing.

Swimming in the Pacific Ocean in Puerto Vallarta, which forever hooked me on the Pacific Ocean. Nearly five decades later I still live close by.

The *Auch Arauch* song which involved walking barefoot in our pajamas over a cobblestone street to go get a midnight snack. (I'm sure it was more like 7:30 pm.)

Every little thing they did, their madness and their love.

Every little thing I remember.

You And Me And Bacon

I don't like bacon.

Let me tell you what makes me supremely cool.

If you ever sit next to me at an establishment where bacon is served, you can have both your share and mine.

Who Pays For Dinner On A Date?

When I was growing up in Mexico, it was scandalously uncouth for the woman to pay.

(I haven't dated in Mexico for over 20 years so I don't know if things have changed on this front.)

When I worked up the courage to start dating in the US (after not dating in over two decades), I preemptively decided I'd split the bill.

It made me feel like I was taking care of myself, and like this way there were no strings attached.

Also, since I was dating online, I reasoned it was more two people agreeing to meet, rather than one of us inviting the other. Expecting the guy to pay seemed almost entitled. I mean, why?

Finally, I felt it was the correct thing to do if I wasn't planning on seeing someone more than once.

The first time I went out with The Man Currently Known As Boyfriend, he had a drink and I had dinner and he insisted on paying despite my protests.

I found this incredibly chivalrous.

Boyfriend and I have been together for almost five years and we split all of our expenses halfway, like the equals that we are.

Sometimes he'll invite me somewhere and insist on paying, which delights me; and sometimes, unbeknown to him (*muahahahaha*) I will take him out on a date and refuse to let him pay.

It makes me feel both cunning and dexterous.

Transition

I adore traveling — once I'm on the road I feel so alive — but paradoxically I don't like leaving my house.

Travel — that specific transition that requires that I walk out the door of my sweet, sweet apartment and lock it behind me — makes me anxious.

It's not that I'm afraid of flying or that I worry I've forgotten something critical that I needed to pack (because I know I have checked off my list 3,543 times).

It's that while my brain understands it's a finite trip my heart doesn't believe we're ever coming back.

I hug Boyfriend tightly.

Me: *"I love you so much! I will always love you! Thank you so much for loving me!"*

Boyfriend: *"Dushka. You'll be back tomorrow."*

Is Complaining Always Bad?

Close to where I live there is a hill.

At the foot of it there is a labyrinth.

A few times a month I come upon this labyrinth and have been noticing how its outlines are beginning to fade.

It made me think how the world tends towards chaos rather than order and how some day soon there would be no trace of it.

Except today I saw a man in a green shirt.

I watched him kick into place every rock. I walked around the hill and came back and he was still at it.

We can complain or lament or have wistful thoughts or we can get up early on a Saturday morning and put things back where they belong.

Sunday

On a perfect Sunday I would read.

I would color.

I would nibble on delicious things and review important reminders we've affixed to our refrigerator.

I'd make tea and pour it into a cup that fit snug in my hands.

I would leaf through the books on my coffee table.

And I would make time to nap. I've had insomnia all my life and my sleep is always disrupted.

To me, a nap is the ultimate luxury.

Before napping I'd dab delicious smelling balm on my lips, cuticles, elbows and feet.

I have a thing for balms that come in tins.

I'd scribble in my notebooks.

I would organize something.

Maybe I'd make sure my top-secret stash of notebooks was lovingly stacked.

Boyfriend would come home late Sunday night.

Him: *"Have you been home all day?"*

Me: *"Yup."*

Him: *"All alone?"*

Me: *"Yup."*

Him: *"What did you do all day?"*

Me: *"Nothing."*

Gentle Dad

One of the big pillars of my upbringing was that my parents raised us religionless.

This absence of religion was a frequent subject of conversation and mattered a great deal to them.

One day my Dad and I were on a plane. I was maybe seven years old.

I was looking out the window and turned to him and inexplicably blurted *"I can't believe how beautiful God made the world"*.

He looked startled and paused. He then grinned and held me close.

This incident reminds me of how lightly he treaded to avoid squashing anything he considered worthy of preserving. Even when it flew directly against what he had intended for me.

You Can't Make This Up

My then husband and I had just bought a house and were standing in our new kitchen.

We noted that the kitchen counters were taller than we were used to.

I was washing dishes and he was chopping vegetables and I felt a grand, tickling sneeze build up.

I took a deep inhale and threw my head back.

Then, gifted with a discreet flair for the dramatic, I covered my nose with my hand and swung forward with the full force of my whole back, hinging at the hips.

"AAAAACHOOOO!"

I brought my chin crashing down on the counter and fell onto the floor.

I lay there crying and laughing and when I tried to explain what had happened I was slurring my words so my husband scooped me up and drove me to the hospital.

I had a purple bump on my chin that looked so terrible they separated us when we arrived.

I had no idea what was happening until I understood they wanted to figure out if he was being physically abusive.

After a few minutes the doctor came by and sat right in front of me.

Her: *"You are in a safe place here. Do you understand?"*

Me: *"Yesh."*

Her: *"I want to run some tests but first I want to hear what happened."*

Me: *"I threw my head back to sneeze and swung forward bashing my chin on the kitchen counter."*

Her: (Long pause)

Her: *"You know what? I believe you. No one can make up something that absurd."*

Look At Me

Today it seemed to me everyone was looking at their devices.

On the bus. People staring down at their phones while walking, trusting others would watch where they were going to move out of the way.

I was grazed by people who didn't even break stride.

I shared meals with friends who set their phones on the table face up, as if their life was taking place on the screen and I was the distraction.

I'm right here.

Boyfriend tends to do one thing at a time but sometimes he comes home and needs to work.

Look at me, I want to say to everyone.

Look at me.

Perhaps it's self-centered to be seen-starved but after feeling like I hadn't been looked at all day this was my diagnosis.

If I, content with being mostly by myself, feel this way I bet others do too.

I need to put down my devices. I need to stop staring at my phone while I walk. Who have I accidentally grazed without breaking stride? Which of my friends have felt non-existent, like distractions, when I ignore them to glance at my screen?

How many times has Boyfriend stood there thinking *look at me*?

I realize it would be creepy to walk the world resolving to meaningfully stare at complete strangers but I can certainly take care to notice the people that I love.

The First Time I Got Drunk

When I was around 14 years old a friend and I saw a movie where everyone got drunk and seemed to enjoy it.

It made me very curious.

I invited said friend over to my house and grabbed a bottle of whiskey from the bar.

We had absolutely no idea how to get drunk. I thought the effect would be instant so we took a shot.

"Feel anything?"

"No. You?"

"No."

"Want another?"

"I guess!"

After that I don't remember anything.

My Mom is shaking me awake. *"WHAT HAPPENED OH MY GOD WHAT DID YOU DO?"*

Then I don't remember anything.

Then, my Mom nursing me and me crying and saying goodbye.

I was sure I was dying.

"This is called a hangover, honey. You want to die, but, guess what? You won't."

The memory of this incident made an abstainer out of me. I very rarely drink, except for an occasional glass of champagne to celebrate something.

The smell of whiskey still makes me shudder. It's been decades.

(I'm sorry I got drunk and threw up everywhere Mom.)

Coloring Books

Coloring is delicious.

It's creative. Not just what I am doing in the coloring book but what I am doing to my brain. I am giving it a break from everything it ever gets to do.

It's a form of meditation if I focus on coloring and let everything else just stay where it belongs (in the past, or in the future).

Coloring isn't goal-oriented. It's not a chore. I don't need to hurry or "do it right" or "finish".

Coloring is the art of doing nothing.

A colorful, dazzling, enchanting nothing.

It's Not Him. It's Me.

I am walking into the kitchen, carefree.

That's when I spot it.

Boyfriend's old gray t-shirt crushed under the sofa cushion.

"Why does he leave clothes everywhere? Why does he expect me to clean up after him? Why must I — " wait a minute.

This is my soft old gray t-shirt. I left it here last night.

I throw it into the hamper.

Boyfriend and I live alone together. Whatever happens around here happens for one of two reasons: either I make it happen, or he does.

So, if it wasn't me, it can only be one other person.

Except that when I'm certain it was him, it's almost always me.

Take the bed. Boyfriend sleeps like a lion, like a man without a conscience, like a rock. I tell him he destroys the integrity of the bed by tearing out the sheets, rolling them into a ball and pushing them with his big feet down to the bottom of the bed.

He looks at me clueless because, you know. He was sleeping.

So there I was the other night, tossing, flipping, restless, fidgety. I'd turn to look at him snoring, still and angel-like.

That's when with horror I deduced the monster sheet crumpler is me.

Me: *"You are so noisy! I can't sleep with you rummaging around in the kitchen like a raccoon!"*

Him*: "Dushka. Can you sleep on the nights I'm not here?"*

Me: *"Well, it depends on the night. But your deafening racket certainly isn't helping."*

Him: *"You are the lightest sleeper on the planet. If a butterfly gently flapped its wings in Japan it would wake you up."*

The next day Boyfriend leaves for a business trip.

I can't sleep.

And so it goes. He polishes off the peanut butter and when I point it out he shows me he has been eating almond butter.

It was me. I finished the peanut butter.

I boast I run the house like a well-oiled machine, despite his inherent chaos. He opens the refrigerator door and I see that aside from a wide array of different hot sauces and a bag of chia seeds, the fridge is empty.

"You'd go feral if I left for too long," he says.

Don't tell him. Don't tell him, but I would.

Flowers And Song

Mexico City is one of the most exciting cities in the world and every visit should begin with the Museum of Anthropology.

It provides a simple, easy to digest, visually stunning panorama of Mexico's complex Pre-Colombian cultural history.

In this museum you can walk under a bronze fountain that holds in place a dazzling umbrella canopy.

You can pay your respects to Quetzalcoatl, the God of light, represented (among many other things) by a winged serpent.

You can descend into a tomb and see how people were buried with everything they would need for the afterlife.

You can gawk at gigantic sculptures of stone.

You can stroll around a scale model of the Pyramids of Tehotihuacán. (And then make sure you visit said pyramids. The base of the Pyramid of the Sun is larger than the Pyramid of Cheops in Egypt.)

The Museum has beautifully kept gardens with replicas of temples you can find across the country.

Every time I go I discover a beautiful piece I had not noticed before.

The walls around the courtyard boast poetic excerpts from Pre-Colombian literature:

"Is this how I should leave? Like the flowers that withered? Will nothing remain in my name? At least flowers! At least song!"

— *Songs of Huexotzingo*

I Wish I Knew

I set the alarm every evening to get up early the next day.

Then, I lie awake wondering if I set it and check it a few times, even though I know I did.

I wonder how I can unequivocally trust myself.

To stretch, my yoga teacher suggests I find a place between ease and effort. Where is that? I need to know, because I could apply it to everything.

I wish I was a math whiz. I'd inhabit a place where problems could be solved, and where the solution, once found, would work again and again.

Math, circular, predictable, reasonable, poetic, difficult.

I'm comfortable with difficult.

How can the people that I love roam free, untethered by my smothering concern; yet know I am there, unfailing, supportive?

How can I forever separate worry from love, release one, embrace the other?

I learned early on to interpret many normal things — getting sick, needing a nap, needing a break — as signs of weakness.

How can I rewire my brain to find power in the characteristics that make me human?

I understand now that I will lose everything I love. How can I regard this with serenity?

How can I always find beauty in loss?

These are the things I want to be an expert at.

That, and I wish I could play the drums.

Terrible Handwriting

I've always had terrible handwriting.

My whole life I've longed for gorgeous penmanship because I love notebooks and look at the blank pages and wish I could fill them with harmony and beauty.

I ruin them instead.

I scribble furiously and often can't make out what I just wrote.

When I write something for someone else to read (a check! A supermarket list!) I make an effort to make it legible, write slowly, and maybe write everything in caps.

It's definitely not as satisfying.

I feel like I'm not letting my handwriting be itself.

I've learned to love — and celebrate — my illegible scribbles. It makes me feel like my notebooks are harder to hack than anything password protected.

A Torrent Of Words

Where I come from you worked things out on your own.

The notion of telling a stranger intimate things about your life was considered gauche.

The only people who went to therapy were in Woody Allen movies.

Then I started dating Boyfriend and we fought constantly. I couldn't figure it out. Fighting constantly was something I didn't do in previous relationships.

I was exhausted.

Wanting to not fight trumped my skepticism towards therapy. It trumped my reluctance to talk about things I feel protective about, such as how my upbringing might or might not have affected my ability to relate.

We went to counseling because we felt we needed help. Not just for our dynamic as a couple but for ourselves.

I felt a storm raging around in my insides and I wanted to learn how to make it stop.

The sitting room where we talked to the therapist was brown and soft. I filled it with a torrent of words.

I wondered if the posters on the walls would somehow absorb what I said, if I could stop with my sadness the clock by his recliner, if I could turn over the small sculptures on his coffee table with my exasperation.

I cried a lot and Boyfriend sat there looking perplexed and uncomfortable and sometimes angry.

Every time one of us spoke the other listened and offered another view of the same story. Many times it sounded like a whole different story.

If you think you have ever recognized Truth try listening to others who recognized it too and you'll wonder if you all were even in the same solar system.

We drank tea and after every session walked across fields of broken glass trying to adhere to the rules we had been advised to follow.

Except, a few days after we'd wobble to our feet, forget to assess the right moment, forget to calculate if we needed to retreat or advance, forget our narrative discrepancies.

Suddenly we were happy, spoke to each other with kindness, learned to fight fair, felt comfortable discarding minor transgressions, ignoring infractions of inattention or distraction.

We learned to not interpret small things as big things. We cut each other some slack.

To me our previously belligerent hot-headed relationship now feels air conditioned.

Cryptic messages are easily decoded and all my words, formerly heavy with stagnant water, flap freely in the wind, strung lovingly on sturdy clothes lines in airy backyards.

Under the right conditions therapy works.

Most of all it taught me to say yes to getting help.

I will never again feel like I have to figure it all out on my own.

The Universe And How It Plots

I had lunch with a Zen teacher today.

We spoke about The Universe.

Does The Universe conspire to help us?

"Of course not," I said. *"If I am a writer focused on writing I see stories everywhere. This is not The Universe — although it definitely feels that way."*

"This is the power of my own attention."

"But Dushka," the Zen teacher replies. *"You are The Universe. The power of your own attention and The Universe assisting you are one and the same."*

Shift In Perspective

My parents separated when I was three and officially split up when I was five.

After divorcing my Mom, my Dad remarried several times.

My relationship with my father's women was odd. There was this ever present, jealous tension that I never knew quite what to do with.

I wasn't "another woman". He wasn't my lover. He was my father.

And the house that they were moving into wasn't a place I visited. It was my home.

Them wanting to "make the house their own" always felt displacing to me, invasive, even predatory.

And, what about feeling that I was in the way?

What could I have done with myself?

I often think I should have handled that whole dynamic better.

Then I remind myself that I was six.

Fast forward to my mid-twenties.

My best friend in the whole wide world falls in love with an older man who has three children from a previous marriage.

Their relationship begins to get serious, and things get difficult.

She comes over to my house, sobbing. My best friend.

"It's so hard, Dushka," she says. *"He loves his kids. They always come first. I feel like I don't ever have a place."*

My brain spins inside my skull. I stand there with my mouth open.

"He asked me to move in with him, but it's like there is no room for me. It won't ever feel like my house. I love him so much. What should I do?"

My perspective was shifted so violently I couldn't speak.

I now methodically, deliberately attempt to put myself in the other person's shoes.

Does Lust Cloud Your Judgement?

A few jobs ago my then boss walked into my office and requested that I be involved on a project that made no sense to me.

I explained why I felt what he suggested would not be helpful and he asked that I do it anyway.

As I assented I felt a flash of anger so strong it clouded my vision.

When I was young, anger came mixed with shame but later it set itself free and felt like a jolt of power, electric and bewitching.

For an instant I longed for a physical altercation, to get up and slam him against the wall.

But I didn't.

There is a bakery near where I live that makes big, fat, oaty cookies with apricot and coconut.

Sometimes I walk by as they are pulling them out of the oven and the only thought in my typically noisy, elaborate labyrinth of a brain is *cookie.*

While succumbing to a cookie is invariably worth it, I have been known to heroically drag my single minded cookie drunk brain and the rest of me home without one.

And then there is lust and the seashell spiral of his ear and the glint of those swampy green eyes and how fun an afternoon would be if I could spend it nibbling the skin on the back of his neck.

We could toss responsibility and replace it with a romp and a frolic and of course my judgment is as foggy as the San Francisco summer sky because my plan is sounding to me like an increasingly excellent idea.

But, alas, my frankly laudable lack of judgment is not good enough of an excuse.

Just because our appetites can yank us around doesn't have to mean we become ungovernable.

Compliment Camp

One scorching hot day wandering across Burning Man I came across a sign that read "Compliment Camp".

Huh.

I peeked in.

"Oh, wow," said a guy standing by the door. *"You have the most incredible hair I have ever seen."*

I beamed. (My hair is SO vain.)

"Whoa, look at her dress," says another guy.

"It's not the dress," the first guy says. *"Look how totally hot this girl is."*

I sat on a dusty red sofa at compliment camp for about 50 minutes. When I walked out of there my ego was colossal and there was a spring in my step.

The next day I could not even approach compliment camp. There was a two hour line out the door.

Burning Man is a gift economy, which means that whatever anyone offers is given away for free. But I bet that out here in the default world many people would be happy to shell out a dollar or two in exchange for a short visit to a compliment booth.

Do We Need Help From Others?

I have no sense of direction.

I don't mean this in a quirky, funny way. I mean it in an impairing way. I don't know where I am and it makes things that are easy for you very difficult for me.

I give myself loads of extra time to get anywhere because I know I will wander around aimlessly for some time.

I was recently trying to get to an important business meeting and I couldn't find the address.

After 45 minutes of walking back and forth within a few blocks I was so frustrated I was ready to call and cancel. Throw in the towel. Give up.

I stood alone on the sidewalk and felt like crying.

How can I be so inadequate?

As a last resort I stopped a stranger. *"Would you happen to know where street number 317 is?"*

She looks up at me, glances at the screen on my phone.

"Your map says it's a block down that way. Here, I will take you."

Here, I will take you sounds to me like someone is gently tossing rose petals over my head.

I check her back to see if her scapula sprout wings.

She walks lightly beside me all the way to the entrance of the building I am looking for.

"Good luck!" She waves and walks off.

I stand there considering two things: that I can't really get anything done without the help of others, and that more often than not what I'm looking for is just around the corner.

Can Love Be A Waste Of Time?

My ex-husband derived a lot of pleasure from extensively researching things before buying them.

He one day decided he wanted to get me a yoga mat. He spent an entire weekend reading reviews and cross referencing relevant information.

While typically he was highly efficient, this time by the end of the day he was in a state of analysis paralysis. He was overwhelmed. He didn't know what to do.

I walked over to his screen and pointed at a mat and said *"Just get this one. I like the color."* I wanted to set him free but I didn't. He required another day before he could make a final decision.

When the mat finally arrived I seldom used it. I liked yoga back then but it wasn't the sanctuary it is now.

Today, after years on that trusty mat, I appreciate it in ways I could not have foreseen.

It's not too heavy to roll up and carry and yet it's thick enough to protect my knees. It's rough so I never slip on it, and it's easy to wipe clean. It has held up well despite the fact I've used it for so long.

It's the perfect mat.

Love is never a waste of time. We give it lavishly, madly, and it studs another person's life with treasures they continue to find in unexpected places long after they are no longer a part of our regular life.

I confirm this every time I roll out my mat and set it down on the smooth wood floor of the yoga studio.

Bucket List

I'm in Mexico visiting my Mom and staying in my old bedroom.

There's the orange carpet and vegetable soup and the house that smells like nutmeg.

We chat and sip sleepy time tea and eat cookies dusted with confectioner's sugar.

We talk about life not like it's snippets (*how was your day?*) but like it's a long arch we can make sense of.

It's like I never left.

It's been three decades.

I've never had a bucket list.

Everything I've ever felt I wanted or needed to do seems to materialize before my eyes.

Superpower

Imagine if every time someone did something annoying, irritating or hurtful you could look at them and feel a rush of love.

Imagine if instead of feeling your insides tighten and coil and lash out in anger or exasperation you could open your heart instead.

Imagine how much you could set down forever: goodbye bitterness, worry, anxiety. Goodbye impatience and hate. Goodbye grudges. Goodbye suspicion. Goodbye fear.

Imagine all the things you could forgive.

Any burden you now carry, anything that zaps your energy, saddens you or exhausts you would dwindle into nothing.

I want Super-Compassion.

Irrational Things I Believe In

I am in my twenties.

Even if you are full, there is a special place in your belly reserved for dessert.

Angels hold early morning strategy meetings to plot how to best protect me.

Boyfriend, and any boyfriend, has never loved another more than me.

I haven't asked. I don't need to.

There are many ways to eat things that make them calorie-free. If you eat a taco standing up, leaning over the sauce pan; or if you munch on broken cookies rather than whole cookies.

This also applies when eating crumbs, and when sharing.

If I am not in Mexico is my Mom's house still there? Does she sit in her chair in the library? I can't be sure.

Things are quickly assembled before my arrival.

For a long time I believed anxiety was a premonition. I am rewiring my brain so that it learns anxiety is just a bunch of thoughts that don't exist unless I make them so.

My Made Up Word

Boyfriend: "*Dushka, do you want more coffee?*"

Me: "*Maybe a smidgen. A tad. A drop. A woonf.*"

Boyfriend: "*A woonf?*"

Me: "*Yeah. It's more than a whiff but less than a dash.*"

We now use woonf for everything.

Activities I Enjoy

I like to flirt. With you and with disaster. Not the ruination kind. The start-over kind.

I like to arrange things so that they look beautiful. It's not OCD. It's a craving for aesthetic.

I like asking why.

I like holding babies, but only for a little while. I like greeting dogs and long to take them home forever.

I like being upside down. A handstand is better than caffeine.

I like beauty products. A face mask. A hair mask. A foot scrub. I like things that smell good. Not flowery or perfumy. Minty, herby, clean.

I like learning.

I like talking to strangers.

I like riding on the bus.

I like travel and all the textures to be found in new, far-flung places.

I like gentle, discreet, respectful eavesdropping.

I like botanical gardens, preposterous looking flora and velvety leaves.

I like looking at you.

I like writing. And editing. And editing. It's not OCD. It's a craving for dactylic rhythm.

I like attention and like being left alone. This is my undoing. This is my salvation.

Fantasy/Desire

My fantasy is to go live in a lighthouse on the coast of Newfoundland.

During the day I'd take long walks along the water on the grassy hills and look out as far as my eyes can see.

I'd sit and listen to crashing waves.

In the afternoons, wrapped in a soft blanket, I'd write and sip tea.

Boyfriend has been to Newfoundland. My fantasy perplexes him. He knows I like warm weather and assures me Newfoundland is too windy and cold for a warm-weather creature like me.

He points out that living in a lighthouse would always be drafty.

My fantasy is to go live in a lighthouse on the coast of Newfoundland, but I don't think it's what I actually desire.

Do Labels In Relationships Really Matter?

Yes please give me labels.

I actually want more than one.

I need one today and another as what we have going on here evolves (or devolves).

I am a fan of clarity.

To me, this is a very big deal.

You see, I don't like the alternative.

I really don't like thinking that I might hurt anyone's feelings if their intentions are different from mine.

I would be adverse to putting myself in a position where I might want something different than what the other person is willing to give me.

The times I have considered dating someone who declares himself opposed to labels I understand and tell him it's fine for him to be label-free.

It just won't be with me.

Prophet

Many years ago, in the days of messenger service and fax machines, my boss asked me to learn how to email so I could teach everyone in the office how to do it.

I told him I'd be happy to, but that in my opinion email would never catch on.

Why would I want to "send an email" to someone who was a door away from mine, or right down the hall?

I've been dead wrong about a lot of things since then, but this one reminds me not to believe everything I think.

Highly Skilled Mechanic

Some day not too far into the future Boyfriend and I will be driving along a very safe road in broad daylight and the car will (gently) break down.

He'll pull over.

We'll be on a beautiful backroad somewhere sunny, maybe with a vineyard or an almond tree plantation.

The trees will be covered with blossoms.

His brow will be furrowed.

"I wonder what happened?"

I'll look over at him at say, *"Don't worry honey. I've got this."*

I will get out of the car, calmly walk around, pop the hood, regard the engine, check on several things that engines have and nod with infinite wisdom.

Then I will saunter to the back of the car, pop the trunk, grab my heavy, complex, well equipped tool belt and after taking some things apart and deftly putting them back together I will fix everything.

"Hey," I'll say *"can you try to start it?"*

He'll turn the key. The car will roar to life.

Then I'll notice that one of the tires is looking lightly deflated and say *"You know what? Let's not chance it. Let me just change this tire."*

Boyfriend's jaw will drop at my smoothness and uncanny car savvy.

Little will he know that just a couple of weeks later I'll fix his motorcycle too.

Why I Like Poetry

Have you ever asked someone to please, just please scratch your back?

There is a place you can't quite reach and are getting desperate and *aaaaaaaah YES. Right there.*

Poetry does this to me. The right poem feels infallible, like clean, perfect aim.

I was so thirsty and needed it so much and now that I see it I feel quenched and I'm sitting here stunned.

Beloved

I am in LA spending time with my family.

A bunch of us went on a beautiful hike.

Then we walked along Santa Monica. It had rained earlier in the day so the sky looked apocalyptic.

After eating so much all weekend it was nice to get a simple lentil salad bowl for lunch.

It had sweet potato and spinach.

In the afternoon we strolled in and out of stores and watched everyone pull down Thanksgiving themed ornaments and put up holiday related ornaments.

It was like witnessing someone fast-forwarding time.

I found roses that looked like candy canes and wanted to take them all home.

In a farewell to the Thanksgiving weekend we spent the evening making cookies and let the kids decorate them.

OK. There was minimal intervention.

I look at my niece and nephew and realize they are old enough to remember.

Their parents who adore them and their grandparents who visit them and their aunt and uncle who try to be a regular part of their life.

There is one thing that I want etched into their brains so through thick and thin it stays there forever: you were loved.

You were loved madly by so many people.

May that stay with you always.

I'm Sorry I Didn't Listen

My father is difficult to explain.

He loved handkerchiefs and Swiss Army knives. He was quirky, proud, private, irrational, impossible. He was full of secrets. He led a compartmentalized life and considered any illness a form of weakness.

When he began showing signs of dementia we didn't speak about it for *years.*

Then we did, in hushed tones.

One day he called to tell me he had cancer. At first I thought he was confused. Then I regarded the cancer as a blessing.

Dementia was fog, illusion, unclear, unreal, untreatable. Cancer was present, concrete. There was surgery. There was treatment.

There was an end.

My father's health declined quickly after this diagnosis but it wasn't a steady decline. He got worse. Then better. Then worse. Then worse than before. Then better.

He lived in Mexico and I lived in San Francisco. I visited as often as I could: roughly every two months. Some visits would make my blood run cold. Others made me wonder if I was imagining everything.

One dark day my brother called to tell me I needed to change my plane ticket to arrive earlier than I had planned. He said my Dad was doing worse. Much worse.

I didn't listen.

I had just spoken to my Dad. He sounded tired and sick but no different than the weeks before.

From one day to the next I called and heard his voice and felt a nuclear bomb go off in my heart.

It was my own internal voice that finally got through to me *DUSHKA GET ON A PLANE GET ON A PLANE NOW TIME HAS RUN OUT.*

Two months before, my father and I had gone out to a restaurant for a late lunch.

This time when I got to Mexico he couldn't stand. He couldn't speak. He was nearly deaf.

The decline over the next few days was meteoric, faster than a free fall. He needed my help to sit up and a couple of hours later I was lifting dead weight.

He was hallucinating.

It was like every function in his body hit its expiration date at the same time.

I made it to Mexico five days before his death. I was in the house with all my siblings and we sat around his bed when he died.

I should have gotten on that plane sooner.

I should have listened to my brother.

I regret most of all putting such a tremendous burden on him; his prudent, tactful voice saying *"move your trip"* and me too distraught and scared to pay attention.

The Best Gift

We were getting ready to watch a movie; my brother, his wife, my niece and I. My niece was around 4.

We sat on a big couch and collected necessary equipment. Pillows, blankets, snacks.

My brother hands me a big bowl of popcorn. He hands my niece another.

He looks at me solemnly. *"Dushka, whatever you do, don't eat her popcorn."*

The movie starts. I munch on my popcorn, finish my bowl, absentmindedly move on to her bowl.

She sees me put my hand on her popcorn and begins to scream.

It doesn't sound like I'm eating her popcorn. It sounds like I'm killing her.

My brother jumps up *"OH MY GOD I TOLD YOU SHE HATES IT NO!"*

Through the years I regularly visit my niece, who is now 8. We're buddies and both love popcorn. She has clearly established with every family member she does not like to share.

Popcorn is hard to come by for her. She has to ask someone to help her make it on the stove top. She cooks quite a bit but needs adult supervision when fire is required.

I recently saw in a store a simple silicon bowl designed to make healthy popcorn from scratch in the microwave oven.

I instantly bought her one and spent about 20 minutes today showing her how, with a bit of caution, she could make her own popcorn.

She freaked out.

She has made popcorn four times today, enough to feed all of us, and got creative with the ingredients and the original recipe I gave her.

She puts oven mitts on to carefully get the big bowl out of the microwave and then beams as she struts around magnanimously providing everyone with an enormous serving of popcorn.

The best gifts I've given are really gifts for myself.

Today I felt like a hero, a genius, the best aunt ever to walk the face of the Earth.

Having It All

When I have been at my lowest, my saddest, my worst —
through illness, the death of a loved one, terror, heartbreak,
shock — do you know what I long for most of all?

Do you know what I realize I've lost that takes the air right out
of my lungs?

Please. Please just bring it back.

It's not privilege or luxury or delight.

It's normal.

I want things to go back to normal.

Bare feet in grass. Getting up out of bed drowsy and reaching for
the glass of water near my bed.

Dinner with friends, simple food, or a bowl of cereal sitting
alone in a comfy chair.

The bus taking too long and being late for work. The grey t-shirt,
my sneakers, the old hoodie I borrowed from him, the red dress
in the back of my closet.

Hitting the snooze button to snuggle. Lifting the sofa to vacuum. The shimmering dust swirling in the slanted light. The crack in the blinds.

Child's pose.

If that's what you have, if your life is normal, just normal, that makes you one of the most fortunate people on Earth.

Having it all really means normal.

One Subject At A Time

Sometimes I am telling Boyfriend about my day and suddenly remember something else I wanted to mention and career off course to start talking about that.

"Dushka," he says, *"you are interrupting yourself."*

Most times this results in him looking at me endearingly but other times it drives him nuts.

He says that due to my excessive enthusiasm I can be very hard to follow.

Truth be told, due to my excessive enthusiasm sometimes I find me hard to follow.

So now when I talk to him I try to focus on one subject at a time.

This proves quite restful for me too.

If I Got A Tattoo

I really like tattoos on other people.

I think about lightly tracing them with my fingers.

I frequently ask strangers to tell me the stories behind their body art.

I don't think I would ever get a tattoo. The notion of injecting ink under my skin feels, perhaps somewhat irrationally, like sacrilege.

Maybe some day.

If I ever did get a tattoo it would almost certainly be a quote.

When my Dad was alive he'd often utter *"Tempus fugit, Dushka. Tempus fugit."* (*Time goes by fast* in Latin.)

On the days before his death he would say, almost to himself, that he couldn't believe his life had gone by so quickly.

The way he'd make this observation, under his breath and looking gaunt and sick and weak, was etched forever into the pit of my stomach.

Tempus fugit.

It would be a small tattoo on my left mastoid bone and would stand as visible evidence of how his whisper — *tempus fugit, Dushka* — rings in my ears.

I'm Forbidden

When I was 16 or 17 years old, a very good friend of mine started seeing a girl who told him she was very jealous of me.

She declared he was "forbidden" to see me.

He agreed.

Before this pact my friend and I used to talk on the phone at least once a day and saw each other several times a week.

We were very close (our relationship was in no way romantic) and suddenly he dropped off the face of the Earth.

I found out a few years later that they had gotten married.

He sent me a note via Facebook a year or so ago — nearly three decades later — using an account that instead of his name had an alias he thought I would recognize.

In this note he told me how much he had missed me all these years, and added that he was happy; that giving up an important friend was his only regret.

He asked if we could be in touch. He couldn't openly "friend" me on Facebook because he didn't want her to see, and asked if we could maintain a correspondence only via Facebook messenger.

It's really not my place to judge or meddle with another person's decisions or another couple's relationship.

But the rules he had outlined for me — *"please write me back so we can rekindle a friendship we need to hide from my wife"* — did not work for me.

I read his note a couple of times and thought *"I'm not touching this."* Then, without responding, I deleted it.

I think of her and think of him and wish them well.

A Few Exceptions

My stellar parents made a big deal out of respecting our privacy, telling us that our room was our kingdom, and staying out of our business.

I always felt I had my own space.

One day I caught my Mom snooping around in my brother's room. I was aghast. Agog. Thunderstruck.

I thought I'd make her jump, confess and squirm in a mire of guilt and repentance.

"MOM NO WHAT ARE YOU DOING?"

She regarded me cool as crisp lettuce and said without a trace of apology *"My son has been coming home consistently late and despite the fact we've talked at length it's my duty to double-check on his wellbeing."*

"Oh my god mother does this — can this mean — ack do you go through my things too?"

"No," she replied.

"With very, very few exceptions."

Turn The Light On

When I read something well written I feel like hugging my book.

I feel like cheering.

I go back and read it again just for the pleasure.

It's almost tactile. I want to run my fingers over well written lines.

If the writer is someone far away from me (for example a book from an author I will never meet) I get all of her books.

If the writer is someone I can contact I always, always encourage.

Please, please write. Don't stop.

I want more writers in the world because good writing is like walking into a dark room and flipping the light switch on.

Elucidate me.

You're In My Spot

In every yoga studio I frequent I have a special spot.

I lay my mat down in the same place every time, away from heating vents, close to the teacher and, if possible, near natural light.

Early this morning I ran into class to find someone was occupying my spot.

There was no one else in the studio.

I walked up to her.

"Good morning! Would you mind terribly moving over a bit?"

"Oh! Yeah! Absolutely! Sure thing!"

I unroll my mat with a gentle thwack, pull out the wrinkles and sit.

Ah. Order is restored.

I feel content.

About 10 minutes later, more awake, more stretched out, brain more refreshed, I realize with dismay I ASKED SOMEONE TO MOVE OVER WHEN I COULD HAVE SET MY MAT DOWN ANYWHERE ELSE ACK!

I'm mortified.

Sheldon Cooper is my alter-ego.

Icarus

If I was kept prisoner

on a beach surrounded by cliffs

and the plan

Implausible

Was to spend my time

collecting feathers to make wings

And one day they were done and I tried them on and incredibly
they fit

And I could fly over the ocean and across the sky

I would not think or listen

I would not be careful or cautious

I would soar towards the sun

would want the heat on my skin

I would stretch out my arms and experience the full span of my
wings

I'd breathe deeply

I would glide

Then plunge willingly into the cool water

Knowing that when I had the power to fly I went all in

and did.

My Poetic Condition

I'm writing this on my phone, flat on my back, trying hard not to throw up.

I was recently diagnosed with Benign Positional Vertigo.

This is so much better than my own interpretation.

I thought I was dying.

Crystals finer than dust were dislodged within the spirals of my inner ear and are floating, misplaced.

I imagine them glittering as they fall, a microscopic scene inside my head similar to dust seen through the slanted light of a window in a darkened room.

The vertigo will resolve itself as the diminute crystals find their way back where they belong.

As the room swirls and I squeeze my eyes shut in search of stability I can't help but notice I have a poetic condition.

Watching the world spin reminds me of my astounding fragility.

Fact: It's glittering dust that keeps our world upright.

My entire life, the people I love and the things I do, my responsibilities and thousands of stories, held up by nothing but resplendent strings finer than cobwebs.

I am tempted to feel humbled that something so insubstantial has felled me.

Except, things knock us over all the time.

This is nothing but evidence of our persistence.

What Do You Think About?

I think about luck.

About good design and how it impacts even the most simple experiences.

I think about beauty and how it sounds superfluous when really we are perpetually searching for some version of it, a slice, a sample, a taste.

It's like power, wearing a mask and a red dress.

I think a lot about how everything is delicately connected and how sometimes I am under the illusion I can catch a flash of all of it and it's wondrous.

I think about how people do completely unexpected things even when you think you have them figured out.

I think how we are always on the edge. Of change, of wonder. Of calamity.

We believe we live in homes when really we live in precipices.

I think about my upbringing and everything my parents gave me, flawed and brimming with love.

I don't think I'd ever learn to distinguish the love from the flaw.

I think about the fact that my Dad was maybe the architect of my inner ear even though he probably never specifically thought about it and now it's too late to tell him.

I think about how maybe he already knows.

How Babies Are Made

My 5-year-old nephew: *"Auntie Dushka, how are babies made?"*

Me: *"It's magic. The magic of creation. And love. And a spark in mommy's and daddy's eyes."*

Him: *"Then what's the vagina for?"*

Firefighter

The first time I went to Burning Man I arrived as Black Rock City was being built.

I witnessed the construction of many of the art pieces, and on the night of the core burn was invited to a platform directly under the man to watch them be set on fire.

The mood was electric, cathartic. Everyone was moving quickly. Boyfriend, who had volunteered to help someone do something, left me standing on the platform.

I looked out onto the desert and saw the sculptures I had climbed earlier that day catch fire.

I cried.

Everyone was yelling, arms up in the air in celebration.

I was inconsolable.

I felt a hand on my shoulder.

"Hey," said a voice. *"Are you OK?"*

I turned around to see a firefighter in full gear. He was wearing a face-mask and an eye mask so I couldn't see his features.

"They — they are burning beautiful things!" I said.

I leaned on his shoulder and cried. He held me for a long while. Then we hugged goodbye.

Two years later I was in my office and my phone rang. *"Hello,"* said a woman. *"I work for a startup and need public relations support. I know this is last minute, but can you meet with my team? Our CEO will be there and we're on a tight timeframe."*

I arrived at this meeting that same afternoon. We did a quick round of introductions, shook hands. The CEO took out his laptop to walk me through the product demo and I saw his screen saver was a photo of The Man burning.

"Oh, you are a burner," I said.

"Yup," he said. *"Have you been?"*

"Yeah. As a matter of fact I'm going again this year. The packing has begun."

"Wait a minute," he says. He looks at me.

"You're her."

I have no idea what he's talking about.

"You cried at the core burn. You said they were burning beautiful things. You hugged a fireman."

I look at him stunned.

"That was me," he says. *"I was the fireman."*

The story could end here and already be hard to believe.

But it doesn't end here.

Two weeks later Boyfriend and I were in the final throes of Burning Man packing. We needed to do one more thing, jump into our van and hit the road.

I grabbed two huge garbage bags and told him I'd swing by the trash room and meet him in the garage.

I ran out of my apartment and down the hall to the garbage room. I see someone walking in the opposite direction, from the trash room towards me.

"Rick?" I'm flabbergasted.

"Dushka?" We stand there.

He finds his voice before I do.

"What are you doing here?" he says.

"I live here," I answer. *"Apartment 2."*

"Dushka," he replies. *"I live in Apartment 4."*

Life is insane. Implausible things happen all the time. Don't let anyone ever tell you differently.

The Mirror

I wake up tired sometimes, stiff and faithless, and there she is.

Her hair sticking out every which way.

We're going gray.

I look at her. She looks at me. We smile.

Long past others who we thought would stay have left, we're still here.

We need others. It's not that.

It's that at the end of the day, it's you and me.

Whoa that was cool, she says when I make her proud.

Oops. That did not go so well, she says when I do something we knew would be a terrible idea.

We might groan at our lack of patience and occasional bad judgment but have each other's backs just the same.

I love the woman in the mirror.

There's nothing perfect about her, and that is my favorite thing.

Words In Spanish That I Need In English

Here are some concepts in Spanish that don't exist in English:

Pinche — multipurpose swear word to use when qualifying something as petty, miserly, stingy, cheap or less than what you expected.

Sobremesa — the time that you spend sitting around the table after a meal, not really eating but maybe sipping and talking.

Mandilón — a guy who is super dedicated to his girlfriend, more so than to his friends.

Estrenando — the very first time you wear something you are *"estrenando".* This is why in the school yard other people stomp on your brand new shoes. That's called *"estrenón".* (Sigh)

Pena ajena — when someone does something that makes you feel a sort of disembodied embarrassment. If I went to a social gathering with my Mom she used to wrap up a slice of cake to take home to my brother. *Qué pena ajena!*

Nimodo — the closest translation I can think of is "oh well". It's like throwing your arms up and saying "this is how things turned out and there's nothing we can do about it." In terms of attitude, it's similar to someone asking you why you did something and you replying with "because". It's not hopeless. It has a certain dignity.

Empalagada — this is how you feel when you've had too much of something sweet. No more chocolate, please! After eating half the box I feel *empalagada.*

If a couple is smooching next to you and saying adoring things to each other after a while you are like, please, ugh, *me estan empalagando.*

A somewhat related concept is *enchilada,* which means you've had too much spicy food and you can't eat anymore, pass the water. Or the milk. Or something with ice. Then pass the salsa and the *chilitos toreados.*

Chile toreado is when you take a spicy pepper and roll it in your hands before slicing it to make it spicier.

The distinction between *amar* and *querer.* Translation for both in English: "to love". In English you use the same word for your feelings towards a lover, a brand of lip gloss and your Mom.

If someone is your *tocayo,* they have the same name you have.

On a perhaps tangential note, Mexicans have a very complicated relationship to the word "mother".

En la madre is like saying "holy shit!", *ni madres* means "no way", *no tienes madre* kind of means "you have no shame", *a toda madre* means "totally awesome!", *esto es una madre* means "this is a piece of shit".

Que poca madre! means "you bastard!", and I could go on, *pero, vale madres,* which means "it doesn't matter".

Parking Karma

Boyfriend is convinced he has what he calls "parking karma".

I have been dating him for five years and can confirm that most of the time we park right in front of where we are going, regardless of the neighborhood, in a city known to be parking challenged.

The fact that he's convinced he's going to find a spot means his eyes are wide open, completely expecting he will find something, rather than closed off in frustration that there is no way.

When others say *"Let's just take a cab so we don't have to park"* he says *"I'm going to drive because I'm going to find a space immediately".*

When others park five blocks away because *"there is no way they will find something closer",* Boyfriend drives right by the main entrance, expecting to find a space there waiting for him. (He usually does. Needless to say, others don't. You can't find what you have given up on.)

Rumi suggests you live your life as if everything was rigged in your favor.

What does this imply?

That you stress a lot less.

That you approach things with optimism.

That you are open and perceptive to notice things you would not see if you thought getting them was simply not possible.

It means that you react to everything you get with a rush of gratitude.

Boyfriend's infallible parking karma is proof of the power of his own perception.

Is the whole universe rigged so he can find a parking spot?

He seems to believe that it is.

Onomatopeia

My favorite words — or the ones I have the most fun with — tend to be onomatopoeic.

I like their good cheer, their humor and infallibility.

They're like toys, but they strike. I think they have thwack.

They feel like a romp, but are as effective as a satisfying click.

I like the flutter and the fling, the gasp and the whiff and the bang.

The chatter and the clanging and the clapping and the buzz. The clucking and the cough. The gargle, the grunt, the hack. The murmur and the patter and the plop. The rattle and the rustle, the sizzle and the slurp, the strum, the thud, and the whisper.

Let's pause for a second and look at zoom. I can't believe it's a word. I insert it in a sentence as often as possible.

Three hurrays to anything that sounds exactly like what it means.

Creep

Two guys are talking next to me at a restaurant.

Guy 1: *"Dude, how do you decide if you take her to her place or your place?"*

Guy 2: *"It depends on how rough I want sex to get."*

Guy 1: *"What do you mean?"*

Guy 2: *"Well, if I get rough and we're at her place, she kicks me out and I have to go home in the middle of the night. If we're at my place, the girl can leave and I'm already in bed."*

Beautiful Body

My mom tried to get pregnant for years before she got pregnant with me.

She claims that the first time I got a mosquito bite she cried for a week.

"I brought this absolutely flawless baby into the world," she says, *"and now it had a blemish, however infinitesimal."*

I've done quite a bit to myself since then. I have hurt nearly every part of me, broken bones, torn tendons, pulled out splinters, experienced abrasions and cuts and scrapes and suffered countless times from every form of heartbreak.

I've seen gaping, bleeding cuts close up and turn to scars and then for the most part disappear.

I shattered my arm in a car accident. Back then the doctor said I could lose it.

I do handstands now.

My arm and I, inverted, wink at each other.

I have heard like a whip, merciless, the sound of my heart crack clean. It was so bad, this blow, that I am pretty sure it's still broken.

And yet, it loves.

Just a couple of weeks ago I experienced a spell of vertigo so severe I silently wondered if life would ever be the same. I stumbled around for days, unable to get from my couch to my kitchen.

How is it that I ever stood upright?

I wrote lying on my back holding my phone as I tried not to throw up.

Today in yoga I tentatively flung my head into forward folds and even ventured into a shaky forearm stand.

I love every millimeter, every cell of this body. It fills me with wonder. It's more resilient than I am.

It's nothing short of miraculous.

But, perhaps more importantly, where else would I put me?

Tectonic Consequences

Have you ever heard of The Butterfly Effect?

It is a theory that sustains that an infinitesimal disruption somewhere can result in massive consequences somewhere else.

It's called "The Butterfly Effect" because it was originally explained with a beautiful metaphor: a butterfly gently flapping its wings somewhere could result in a hurricane in another location at another time.

A flap of the wings of a butterfly.

Even if it's true that we are indeed insignificant, even if it's true there is no life after this one, your small acts and decisions can have tectonic consequences.

Graves' Disease

I was diagnosed with Graves' Disease right around the time I turned 20.

The diagnosis came as an immense relief because I had been experiencing for quite some time a whole host of symptoms that made me feel like I was losing my mind.

Never underestimate our ability to get used to things we should not ever be tolerating.

Given the time, we can regard almost everything as "normal".

For context, I am by nature restless, energetic and fidgety. I've always had difficulty sleeping and am prone to anxiety.

The symptoms of Graves' Disease were masked by the fact they mimicked my personality, so making a distinction between the disease and me took many years and a gigantic stroke of serendipity.

Before I knew it, I was always hot, even when it was cold out. I was always hungry, eating full meals less than an hour after a meal and calling it a "snack".

I felt shaky and anxious and couldn't sleep more than a couple of hours at a time.

My muscles felt weak and my eyes had trouble focusing.

My heart would race and I felt irritable, moody.

People near me thought the symptoms were consistent with an anxiety disorder.

My Mom suggested we go see a psychiatrist.

I was reluctant because it just didn't feel like anxiety fit what I was feeling. Anxiety lives in my brain and whatever this was was living in my body.

One day, my Mom and I went to visit one of her friends. I think we were supposed to pick something up.

When we arrived her friend mentioned her son was home from college. He was a medical student.

She called him into the living room to introduce us. He walked in, honey-eyed, big-nosed, shaggy-haired and lanky.

We looked at each other.

He extended his hand out to shake mine.

"Do you like books?" he asked, instead of *"pleased to meet you."*

"What? Books are my very favorite thing!"

"Well, come upstairs then! I'm storing my books in boxes. I might even give you some."

We went upstairs and I helped sort his books. We chatted, and I could hear myself talking a mile a minute. My words were wild horses.

He asked if I wanted to go grab a bite. *"Just to be clear,"* he said *"I'm asking you on a post book sorting date."*

We went out for dinner and I was bouncing off the walls. I sat there on a cold evening with a t-shirt on, feeling flushed. I ate my meal and most of his.

He was staring at me the whole time, entranced.

I felt bewitching.

I didn't expect what he said next.

"Dushka, Dushka, Dushka."

"Yes?"

"You need to go get your thyroid checked."

"What?"

"I think you have Graves' Disease. A blood test would confirm my suspicions."

I did some research on later that night and cried when I read the list of symptoms. What a relief. They described exactly how I had been feeling.

I went to get a blood test the next day, which confirmed my thyroid levels were through the roof.

It took a year or two to finally land on the right treatment and medication but I haven't even thought about the fact I have Graves' Disease in decades, except for the times I get blood tests to make sure things are where they should be.

Yes, Go

A long time ago I dated a guy who threatened to break up with me every time we had a fight.

It was so stressful and sad and made me feel like nothing I did was good enough.

One day, exhausted, I called his bluff. He said he wanted to break up and I agreed.

He then admitted that this had never been what he intended but by then it was too late.

I was ready.

He had spent a year preparing me.

Fading Friendships/Forever Friendships

Back when summer was like a whole, entire lifetime my Mom took me on a two month trip and when I came back my best friend had another best friend and no time left for me.

Or, the friend who got a serious boyfriend and every weekend they drove to the house his parents owned on a lake.

Or when I was the one to meet someone, which altered the cadence another friendship had grown used to and come to expect.

Or, when this other friend of mine and I, we were both barely 16, and she started dating a guy in his thirties, long before this had a name and was considered a crime.

The first time they had a fight he threw over the wall of her house hundreds of roses to get her to forgive whatever it was he did.

She said that despite it all he made her feel like a princess and that I wouldn't understand.

They had a fairy tale wedding and she quickly became a stranger. We didn't have much to talk about after that.

When they sometime after got a divorce it was hard to relate to the things she had gone through.

We were nineteen.

There was the guy friend whose girlfriend requested he stop seeing me. This is likely to dent any friendship.

And the other guy friend who decided not hanging out with me now that he was dating someone was for the best.

It's nature's course for some friendships to grow apart.

On the other hand I have friends who I don't see for years and we pick up where we left off; as if absence and distance were just an illusion and our relationship was the thing that was real.

Friends who become moms whose kids call me auntie. They run to the door to hug my legs when I get to their house.

Friends who get married and invite me over for dinner. I sit at their table and pass big platters of food around and fake-argue with their children over the biggest slice of cake.

One of my best friends is pregnant. I talk to her unborn girl in Spanish.

I whisper to her that one day when she's a teenager and wants to get away from her parents she will have a place to run to.

"En mi casa siempre tendrás tu casa, mi amor."

It's nature's course for some friendships to grow and become more like family.

Anniversary

Boyfriend and I met in the lobby of a hotel bar.

I had read his online profile and expected the evening to be a lot of fun.

I think he went on the date with me because he had enjoyed the banter of our correspondence.

Our first date was light and we laughed a lot but it also had a certain weight. I don't believe in The One or in the self-deception of "love at first sight" but I do think we proceeded deliberately.

I always knew we were very different and anticipated the relationship would never be easy (I was right) but immediately I liked his character, the silver hair and his big nose.

Our anniversary is the day we met because after that date I went out with other people and all I could think was *"you're not him."*

Show-Off

When I was born, my Mom spoke to me in English and my Dad in Spanish.

I have never spoken or thought in just one language.

When I turned 17 I spent a year in France, learning how to speak French. It's been a while so my French is rusty (to put it mildly) but a few days of full immersion in a French speaking country refresh the French speaking part of my brain.

After that I lived in China for over a year, studying Mandarin full time at the Beijing Language Institute. I was never fluent but could bargain in a street market, crack a few jokes and catch enough of a conversation to give people the impression I understood more than I did.

Or, did I understand a lot more than people thought I did?

We'll never know.

Today, my Mandarin is way more than rusty. It's a disgrace. That being said, I can still say hello and goodbye and I love you and other important things.

I met an Italian man when I was in my late twenties and married him. (The fact that he spoke Italian was not the only reason.) We were married 15 years and spoke Italian at home, so my Italian is good enough that Italians ask me what part of Italy I'm from.

I adore languages and have a tendency to pick up words when I visit other countries. I can say hello and please and thank you almost anywhere I go, and learn how to order local delicacies and other carefully selected juicy morsels of my favorite dishes. Most of the time, locals tell me wide-eyed that I have an excellent accent.

This has gone straight to my head and made a terrible show-off out of me so now instead of impressing Boyfriend with my evident language prowess he rolls his eyes and sighs.

Just Three Words

If my currently wordy life was limited to three words, I'd want these to place me on a path of ever increasing adventure and continuous improvement.

Yes. Yes to possibilities, serendipity, discovery, experience and enterprise. Yes to curiosity. Yes to chance.

Yes I want to try that, taste that, go there, do that. Yes, please.

Then, I would want a word to give me a better view of the world, a more fortunate perspective and healthier vantage point.

Thank you. Thank you for my good fortune. Thank you for giving me so very much. So much. Why me? I don't know, but thank you.

Thank you for the lessons you have placed before me. Thank you for my parents and for pears, for effort and for illness, for fear and circumstance and love. Thank you for insomnia.

Thank you for the ability to walk away. Thank you for the ability to stay.

Homesick

The word "homesick" does not exist in Spanish. You can say "I miss my home" or that you are feeling "nostalgia", even "melancholy", but it's not a handy, right on the mark, single word like it is in English.

This is proof that you can indeed feel what you don't have a word for.

What exactly is "home"? When you leave your country of origin to go to another, when does the place you go to become home, if ever?

Are immigrants destined to feel forever incomplete, harboring a vague sense of loss, of not belonging, a disorientation that lingers for years?

Do these people dream of one day returning only to realize that ten, twenty years have gone by, that their lives have been accidentally built elsewhere, that what they knew as "home" no longer exists?

I tend to make home wherever I am. I don't mean that I have no roots, but rather that I grow them quickly. Personal space is important to me, so I swiftly create and inhabit it.

I seldom suffer from homesickness, unless I'm traveling on business, in which case all I want is to return and walk around the house touching my things, doing laundry and making soup.

To me, home is California. Writing this almost makes me feel like a traitor. I was raised to love my country. I was supposed to miss it forever.

It has happened, though: I'm homesick for California when I am in Mexico.

I tell myself that California used to be Mexican territory. Can I be blamed for circumstantial political geography? Am I not, strictly speaking, on Mexican soil?

You don't have to answer that.

Are Women Afraid Of Men?

This past April (2016), Catalina Ruiz-Navarro, a Colombian writer and activist, issued on her Twitter account a chilling, courageous invitation.

"When and where was the first time you were sexually accosted? We all have a story. Make yourself heard using the hashtag #miprimeracoso."

What happened next was absolutely staggering.

Hundreds of thousands of stories poured in.

Because she specifically requested *"the first time"* most of the incidents shared took place when the women who wrote them were little girls.

Her hashtag remained the trending topic for some time.

Fact: Nearly every woman has a story.

It would be imprecise for me to tell you I am afraid of men.

But I can say I have never met a woman who hasn't at some point in her life felt like prey.

Space, Uninterrupted

I need space.

In cities I need a place where my eyes can see as far as they can, uninterrupted by walls and buildings and structures.

I live in a city.

I feel I need a whole ocean to float on. A swath of sky so I can lie on my back on the grass and see the clouds blow by.

Sometimes I feel crowded by others, by their demands and their neediness and their clinging and their noise.

When I feel this way it's hard to find solace.

"Why won't everyone just give me some space?"

Here is the thing I grew to realize. That this requirement — and every other requirement — is something I need to manage for myself and not something anyone can give me.

There Is No "Should"

Boyfriend and I are very different and our relationship improved and became less strained when I let go of the notion that doing everything together was a requirement.

We both have many different interests and tastes that don't always overlap.

He likes reunions more than I do and often goes to dinner parties without me. He is happy to be with his friends and I am happy to be at home.

I have groups of friends he is not a part of who have never even met him and frequent restaurants where I know he wouldn't like the food.

I spend a lot of time alone or share it with other people, which means that my life has become richer and more varied rather than increasingly circumscribed to a single other person.

When we are together we know it's because we want to, and because we both enjoy whatever it is we are doing.

We support and encourage each other and always have something new to talk about.

We have developed our own relationship, not a relationship forced into the shape of how things "should be".

Stoic

I worry that I'm a terrible patient.

I've had a nasty cold for the past ten days and worked through every one of them, including travel and late night flights.

I finally broke down and went to the doctor yesterday and am now on antibiotics and bed rest with an acute bronchial infection.

I should have paid attention to the shortness of breath, the burning feeling in my throat, the nausea, the fever and the incessant coughing that kept me awake despite my exhaustion.

It's just that I love what I do and didn't want to miss it.

Now I have no choice but to lie here and wait it out.

I aspire to be the very image of stoicism but instead moan and cough through the night.

During the day I cry and tell Boyfriend I'm dying.

Boyfriend = saint.

Post-Apocalyptic Swampy Eyes

I marvel at how a woman can write about a boy who is really a sorcerer if she has never been a boy and has never practiced witchcraft.

I wonder how a man can write horror stories about ghosts who have never haunted him.

I can only write about things I have experienced. If it hasn't happened to me I don't know how to approach it or describe it.

I've tried, of course. It's just that if I haven't lived through it, makes my writing sound like tin.

A friend once asked if I ever had writer's block. How could I, if I can walk down the street any time?

Someone with a wondrous, often twisted sense of humor took all the secrets of life and hid them behind see-through sleights of hand.

I need life experiences to write.

Other writers have instead given us life on interplanetary space ships and visions of our existence on Earth after the apocalypse.

In that post-apocalyptic experience I would still scavenge to find time for myself. I would meet a guy with swampy eyes who'd say he likes my hair.

During the day I'd assemble a covert army dedicated to ensure the people I love are safe.

Then I'd hunker down at night and write about how once my nights were rich with stars.

I would write about how despite all the destruction I love this world still, and find it so beautiful, despite all the scars.

Matchmaking Is My Jam

A friend of mine had recently broken up with her boyfriend.

"I'm so tired of the dating game," she told me. *"So tired. Do you know what I want Dushka? I just want a friend. A friend! Someone I can go to the gym with. That's it. I don't think that's a lot to ask."*

A couple of days later my then husband invited a co-worker over for dinner. He had recently ended a relationship.

"I am so frustrated," he told us. *"Why is everything so complicated? All I want is a companion. Someone I can do simple things with. Like, go to the gym. Is that so hard?"*

I suddenly felt like life had placed before me everything these lovely people were so desperately asking for.

How could I turn my back on this kind of serendipity?

I set them up on a blind date and they got married less than a year later.

Bigger Than Me

A few weeks ago I was up in the Marin Headlands taking in a spectacular view of the Golden Gate Bridge.

There was a couple there taking selfies.

I offered to take a photo of them and they declined.

They took a bunch of pictures and came over to show me the results. I could see them making various very, very cute faces, but I couldn't see the jaw-dropping view behind them.

They could have taken these photos in their living room.

I don't understand selfies.

I would much rather step back to see I am a part of something wide and open and beautiful and much bigger than me.

Finders Keepers

I must have been around 15.

I was having dinner at a restaurant and I got up to go to the bathroom. I went over to the sink to wash my hands and right next to the soap dish I saw it.

A big, beautiful diamond ring.

It was so shiny.

I slipped it on my finger.

I wanted to keep it.

The door slammed open.

I put my hands in my pockets.

A woman ran into the bathroom *"OH MY GOD DID YOU HAPPEN TO SEE A RING MY ENGAGEMENT RING I LEFT IT BY THE SINK DID YOU SEE IT?"*

I took a breath *goodbye beautiful ring* and gave it back to her.

She threw her arms around me, hugged me so tight she lifted me off the floor.

One evening many years later I met a man currently known as Boyfriend. We had a really fun first date and then another and shortly after that I looked at him and thought *mine. He is mine.*

I wanted to keep him.

We have been together for years and in that time I have learned that while I love him and he loves me he doesn't belong to me.

He sometimes hugs me so tight he lifts me off the floor.

You know that saying "finders, keepers?" It's rarely true.

What I wish for myself, and for you, is that you regard the poetry present all around you with open palms.

Nothing is yours to keep.

That's what makes it beautiful.

Call Me Every Day

Me: *"Dad, I'm going on a business trip so won't be calling you for a few days. I just wanted to let you know so you wouldn't worry."*

Dad: *"Oh. No phones where you are going?"*

Me: *"I'll just be really busy."*

Dad: *"I am very worried that you are working too hard."*

Me: *"Dad! No! Ack! Don't worry!"*

Dad: *"Call me every day just so I know you are doing ok."*

Me: *"OK. OK!"*

Sigh.

Does Everything Have An Explanation?

There's this coffee shop I walk by every day that is roomy and sunny and has high ceilings. It's such a beautiful space but it's poorly designed. It's almost impossible to find a place to sit.

When you do find one, those sitting around you are too close because of a continuous bench up against the wall, so meeting friends there is inconvenient as it's not really possible to hold a private conversation (or chat without bothering others).

Getting there early and grabbing a spot to sit in with your computer doesn't work either because there are no plugs available to recharge your devices.

"How could a recently opened coffee shop have no plugs?" I ask Boyfriend. *"I don't know what they were thinking."*

"Dushka," he says. *"That coffee shop is perfectly designed."*

If customers can plug their devices they can order one coffee and stay for the day.

This results in minimal consumption but exorbitant electricity bills.

This coffee shop is beautiful and encourages people to walk in, order, and walk right out with their drinks once they realize staying is not as comfortable as it seems.

"Wow," I realize. *"I was looking at that completely wrong."*

"It's not so much that you were wrong," Boyfriend says. *"It's about perspective. The shop was designed by the owners, not the customers."*

I think everything has an explanation. It's just that we are not always standing in a place where we can see it.

My Superhero Cape

When I visit my niece and nephew I place a superhero cape in my suitcase.

I ring their doorbell and they run over to welcome me, then dash into the guest room to watch me unpack.

I pretend to be discreet with the cape, take it out of the suitcase with flair and velocity and hang it in the back of the closet.

"WHAT IS THAT WHAT IS THAT AUNTIE DUSHKA?"

"What? Nothing! Kids. I don't even know what you are talking about."

They spend the rest of the afternoon whispering to each other and eyeing me suspiciously.

Paranoia

Ack. I'm running late and have to get to the airport.

I zip my suitcase closed, grab my bag and run downstairs to hop on my Uber. He drops me off at my gate and I dash to stand in line in security.

I hand the officer my ID and my boarding pass. He looks at my photo. Looks at me. Looks at my photo.

Smiles.

"Good morning, Ms. Zapata! Have a wonderful trip!"

I feel the same way you would feel if someone rested an ice cold hand on the nape of your neck.

"Oh my god," I think. *"How does this complete stranger know my name?"*

Who Is It?

Take it from me

It is possible to forget everything

Your name

It is possible to forget your own language

the most basic words

possible to forget your face

to be startled by a delayed recognition of her reflection on a
window

who is it then who is doing all this forgetting

and how will she a few years from now

manage to locate herself in the world

Not My Responsibility

My parents divorced when I was very little and were both under the impression they completely agreed on how to raise us.

It's true they agreed on the big things, but they didn't on the small things.

For a kid, the small things are the big things.

Watching Saturday morning cartoons was allowed in one house and was sacrilege in the other. Junk food was forbidden in one house and served in the other.

One house was ruled by a Goddess, bewitching and prone to magical thinking; the other by a beloved Dictator who demanded structure and suffered from bouts of paranoia.

I hid from my parents the fact that I struggled to keep track of who I needed to be.

This struggle did not stem from a pandering for approval but rather from craving peace.

I wanted everyone to get along and be happy and they would not be if they found out.

I needed to make sure they didn't find out.

Disagreeing with (or breaking) what was a hard rule in one house and a non-rule in the other felt disloyal and I spent most of my time feeling like I was betraying someone I loved.

Later in life I asked my (many) siblings if they felt similarly and they looked at me like I was completely out of my mind.

Leave it to me to believe I could manage the unmanageable.

It took me years to catch on to what was obvious to everyone but me: that mediating, orchestrating communication and making sure everyone was satisfied and comfortable was not my responsibility.

I have learned to set down many heavy things that no one ever asked me to carry. It's no wonder that the older I get the lighter I become.

Can You Have Your Cake And Eat It Too?

About a year ago I did some research on the saying *"you can't have your cake and eat it too"*.

I mean, why would I want to have a cake and not eat it? It made no sense.

I learned that we are actually saying it backwards.

The original is *"you can't eat your cake and have it too"* meaning that if you've already eaten it, you can't still have it.

Devotion

I am in yoga and feeling frustrated because I woke up stiff and can't touch my toes.

Everyone is doing a forward fold with hands flat on the floor and I can't touch my toes — not even with the tippy tip of my fingers.

My hamstrings are tight and I can't do today what I did yesterday and why does everything have to be so hard?

I go to child's pose and stay there on the floor, taking deep breaths. I don't push my frustration away like I would have. I don't leave the class like I would have. I don't try to escape like I would have.

I sit there in child's pose with all my frustration, painful and caustic and glorious.

And that's when I feel it.

Thank you. Thank you for teaching me about the breath. Thank you for this tool I can use any time. Thank you for making my hamstrings tight. Thank you for this sacred place where I come find myself.

Thank you for a religionless life and a devotional practice.

Is The Letter "N" Negative?

The letter "n" is, like every letter, neutral.

Or I could make the case that it is nice.

N could in fact be the nicest letter.

Look at it. Notice it. It's so nifty and natural. It's necessary. Without it, how could I nap?

I'd have no hope of reaching nirvana.

I would be unable to narrate or navigate.

I'd never meet my neighbors.

It is thanks to this letter that my food can be nutritious and that I too can be nurtured and nuzzled.

Nothing is ever cursed or blessed. It's all in how you choose to look at it.

Catastrophic Thoughts

My insides cannot make a distinction between a fight in a relationship and the end of the relationship.

I understand intellectually that people fight and can (and do) come back from the fight, often stronger.

I understand too that fights allow those involved in the relationship to witness its resilience.

But the whole time the other person is arguing or reasoning or getting angry or doing whatever people do during a fight, I am considering what to pack.

I am planning where I can spend the night.

This makes fighting particularly taxing.

The other person is negotiating, healthy and essential for outlining ever-shifting boundaries.

I am cashing in.

I have learned to manage this sensation of total impending destruction by separating it from me.

It's just a possible outcome and while it could be real it's equally likely that it is not.

"I see you are making sure that we survive no matter what," I tell me. *"Thank you for that. But, let's just wait and see."*

"I know this is frightening Dushka but can you see how you arranging clothes into a suitcase might turn this small incident into a self fulfilling prophecy of relationship obliteration?"

I remind myself that my catastrophic thoughts don't get to decide for me if this relationship will end right now.

This separation has helped me remain calm and not be devastated and see that sometimes someone can find me irritating or difficult and love me still.

Self-Contained Universe

My Mom was born in California and hitchhiked to Mexico in her late teens, never to return.

There she met my Dad and (a few years later) they had me.

From the time I was in her womb she spoke to me in English and he (and the rest of the world, as I was raised in Mexico) spoke to me in Spanish.

I have never known what its like to think or speak in only one language.

Every language holds a self-contained universe. It has its expressions and idioms and way of looking at the world. It has words, and therefore concepts, that don't exist outside itself.

I don't speak Japanese but thanks to my sister I recently learned that there is a word in that language for the type of anxiety you feel after buying books you have not read: tsundoku.

I wish I could learn every language. I think I'd come an inch closer to understanding everything.

Aioli, Drizzled

As much as I like food, if I am alone I don't really think about preparing dinner. Oatmeal maybe, and an apple.

If I'm feeling industrious I might pull out a knife and spread peanut butter on my apple slices.

I recently left on a business trip and came back to find in the refrigerator leftovers of what had recently been a whole, golden, roasted chicken. It was surrounded by delicately browned baby potatoes and root vegetables.

Beside it were two side dishes: sweet potato fries and an oven dish with asparagus.

Me: *"What did you put on the asparagus?"*

Him: *"I drizzled them with a homemade lemon aioli."*

Me: *"Did you just say drizzled?"*

Him: *"Yup."*

Left to my own devices, I (maybe) slice an apple. Boyfriend roasts a whole chicken and makes mayonnaise from scratch.

This is just one of the many reasons I wonder how on Earth I came upon a man like this.

A Bond

I had a dog once who used to look at me with devotion. I thought she was mine but now I think maybe I belonged to her instead; not because she owned me but because I loved her.

There is a difference and it's hard to explain but she understood it.

I was the one who had to catch up.

She was a visitor, this dog, with a soft coat instead of wings. In the time we had together she taught me what a privilege it is to get to love someone so much without expecting anything back.

It's based on this relationship with a strong-chested, four-legged creature that I can say I don't think you can own any other living thing.

You form a bond, and in a way you belong to each other, and that is not the same.

To Improve Your Vocabulary

I think in words. To quote Wittgenstein: *"the limits of my language are the limits of my mind. I don't know what I don't have words for."*

When I write, I do so with a dictionary and a thesaurus within reach. This way, if I want to tell you about an unease I can't quite describe that is more discreet than distress I know I can call it apprehension or disquiet.

When I read, I look up words even when I think I can infer their meaning from how they look or sound. Because vexillology is not the science of annoying or irritating things.

I listen to the radio, watch TV and listen to books on tape. I talk to people who have different areas of expertise. I notice etymology, hoping for clues (when Theseus went into the infamous labyrinth he unraveled a "clew", a ball of string his lover gave him, to find his way back out).

I collect words that cannot be translated into other languages, like *sobremesa* (the time you spend at the table chatting after you are done eating) or *kummerspeck* (the weight you gain when you eat because you are sad. It literally translates into grief bacon).

To expand your vocabulary, read. Write. Look up words in the dictionary. Flip through the dictionary for fun. But mostly, love words. Love them with fervor, with ardor, with vigor, with lust. Love them into the opposite of oblivion.

The Beginning Of The End

I was around fifteen and he was maybe a year older.

On Saturday afternoons he'd pick me up in his father's (stick shift) car and we'd go to the creamery near my house.

Each ice cream cone had a piece of something wonderful at the very bottom: a chunk of caramel, or gummy bears, or a teaspoon of sprinkles.

We'd order and walk out on the sidewalk with our double scoops on sugar cones, sit on colorful folding chairs in delectable silence and eat and look at each other's goofy smile and sticky lips.

When he got to the very bottom of his cone he'd stretch out his hand and offer me that last bite.

"Oh, no, I couldn't," I'd say. I'd try to look aghast and reluctant.

"But you have to," he'd say. *"It's a gift of love. You can't turn down a gift of love."*

So I'd present to him the last bite of my cone.

"Oh, I couldn't," he'd say. He'd look horrified.

"But, what if it is a gift of love?"

We'd swap the last bit of our cones, devour and discuss what the treasure had been. Oh, peanuts! Fudge! A chocolate kiss! Coconut!

One Saturday afternoon I offered him the last precious bite of my ice cream cone. That's when I realized he had already eaten his.

We didn't break up for another few weeks but I knew right then this was the beginning of the end.

A Torrid Romance

I'm walking down the street and two people right in front of me exit a building. They walk over to the side.

"This is why I wanted to talk to you," he says. He looks around, looks back at her. *"My last day is this Friday."*

"What? WHAT? Noooo!" She says. *"Nooooo! Is this because of me? Because of us?"*

I can't even tell you the amount of story endings I have missed by believing it actually matters for me to get where I am going.

The Sounds Of The Jungle

My best friend in the whole world and I hung out every day. We were inseparable. She spent so much time at my house my parents considered her another daughter.

Then she met a guy and I barely saw her.

I felt alone. And hurt.

And bored.

In my head I wrote her off. Friends don't abandon friends. Friends don't completely forget about their friends.

How could she?

Then I stood back and stepped outside myself and realized friendship could not be defined as time spent together but as wishing the other person happiness.

What you want is for your friends to have everything they desire, even when this does not involve you.

Also, her spending time with her boyfriend did not mean she was leaving me. It just meant she was spending more time with her boyfriend.

This is a critical distinction.

We have wished each other well through decades; through awful and fortunate relationships and moving to different countries and getting married and getting divorced and her miracle child and pursuing different interests and assembling different lives and living thousands of miles away from each other.

This friend has context for my life and knows where I come from. She has spent time in my father's library and has sat in my mother's garden. She knows all my siblings.

She met my youngest sister when she was seven. She's now in her early thirties. We wonder how on Earth my baby sister got so old when we are still so young.

Our friendship has become a treasure.

I just spoke to her yesterday. While we talked I looked out the window of my apartment to see the buildings across the street, people walking on the sidewalk at a clip holding their messenger bags and their large coffee cups.

"There are two toucans outside my window," she said. *"They are eating the bananas from the banana tree."*

I could hear behind her the sounds of the jungle.

She said that if one of her work projects falls through it would grant her time to come see me and spend time in a big city.

I miss her but I hope she gets that project. She sounded excited about it.

Name The Band

No matter where we are, no matter what time it is, no matter who is around us, a song comes on and I turn around and yell, *"YO BOYFRIEND NAME THE BAND"* and he always knows.

Always.

Hawt.

Pomegranate Seeds

Persephone was the beautiful daughter of Zeus (king of all gods and rampant womanizer) and Demeter, the goddess of harvest and fertility.

She grew up in a land of perpetual summer, surrounded by gardens and flowers in bloom.

One day Hades, the God of the Underworld, appeared before her. He was struck by her beauty and fell in love with her instantly. He resolved to take her with him to his dark kingdom beneath the Earth.

Demeter searched everywhere for her daughter. She could not find her and as she despaired everything green began to die.

In the meantime Hades showed Persephone his world and offered to make her his Queen. She missed her family and flowers and trees but began to consider how she could make a life of her own here.

She knew that eating anything in the underworld would result in her being unable to leave so she declined constant offerings of food that Hades left before her.

Demeter finally realized where her daughter was and demanded that she be returned. Her father had some influence, so Hades, once discovered, had no choice but to give her back.

As he prepared to travel back to Earth he offered Persephone one last thing: the gleaming, red, jewel-like seeds of a pomegranate. Persephone regarded him as if to say *"I know full well what I am doing"* and after months of eating nothing placed six pomegranate seeds in her mouth. Then, she returned to her mother, and back on the surface of the Earth everything bloomed and flowered once again.

Because of those six pomegranate seeds, Persephone returns to the Underworld six months out of the year, and that is why winter exists.

Whenever I eat pomegranate seeds I think I couldn't possibly blame Persephone for what she did.

The Woman In The Post Office

I went to the post office today to return a package.

The woman helping me was gruff and efficient and brusque.

"Your postage isn't paid for," she said.

"And, when you opened the bag your package came in, you tore it." She sighs. *"I will tape it so you can reuse it."*

Her face was stern and her brow furrowed as she walked around creating my label, restoring the plastic bag and explaining how to run my credit card.

"Hey," I said. *"Guess what? I wrote a book!"*

I took *Amateur* out of my purse and plopped it in front of her.

She stopped. She stared at the book. Her frown disappeared. Her eyes widened. She looked at me, then at the book.

She smiled, so wide and so open.

It was such a stunning, unexpected reaction I felt my eyes tearing up.

"OH MY GOD THIS IS INCREDIBLE I AM SO PROUD OF YOU."

"Do — do you, ummm, want to know why there is a diamond on the cover?"

"Yes," she says. *"YES! Why is there a diamond on the cover?"*

"Well, you have to read the very short story on the back."

She flips the book over and reads the story. When she looks up, she is crying.

Her lips are squeezed together. Both her hands are flat on her heart.

She is shaking her head and looking at me and weeping. I'm weeping.

"You can keep the book," I say.

She gasps. She dashes out from behind the counter and throws her arms around me. We stand there hugging.

"Would you like me to sign the book?"

She looks at me in disbelief and nods vigorously.

I take the book from her and write —

"For the kind of person who changes the course of a stranger's day."

I close it and give it back. We say goodbye. I walk away towards the exit and turn around.

She is still standing there, hugging my book to her chest.

The Recipe For Immortality

When we love we leave a piece of ourselves in the person we are loving or the thing we created with this love.

This cannot either diminish us or put us at risk.

It's precisely the propagation of love that allows us to live forever.

I realize it's all finite.

It's what we leave in others — and what others leave in us — that makes us eternal.

To put it in other words, the recipe for immortality is love.

Disarming Candor

My father had an on-again, off-again relationship with a woman for many years.

When they were happy it was delightful to be in their periphery.

When they weren't, their relationship was combustible, volatile and destructive, not just to the two of them but to everyone around them.

They were married for years, then dated intermittently after their divorce.

One day my Dad called to ask for advice (or, to quote Ambrose Bierce, to seek my approval on a course already decided on).

By now I was in my late thirties and living in another country so the impact his relationships could have on me had dramatically shifted.

"We are thinking of getting back together and you know us so I'd value your opinion," he said.

"Well," I said. *"Have you since the last time you broke up changed in any fundamental way?"*

He paused before answering.

"*No,*" he said. "*No I haven't.*"

(I adored his disarming candor.)

"*Have you observed since the last time you broke up that she has changed in any fundamental way?*"

"*No,*" he said. "*No she hasn't.*"

"*Then you are replicating what you have done in the past and as such can predict the course of what will happen next,*" I said.

"*You don't need my advice. We've all already seen this movie.*"

Our Neighborhood

Boyfriend and I, listless, take an evening walk around the neighborhood.

As we loop back towards home we peek into the new bakery down the street.

"Hi," I say to the hostess as we walk into the beautiful, spacious location. *"We are neighbors. Can we poke around?"*

"Of course," she says. *"Welcome!"*

We ogle the ice cream counter, the big ovens, the meat section.

An employee runs over. *"I hear you are neighbors!"* he says. *"Thank you so much for coming in for a visit. Please accept this gift from us."*

It's impossible not to feel inundated by gratitude while hugging a still warm, crusty loaf of bread.

So Much Better Than My Twenties

In my twenties my emotions — unruly, impetuous, imprudent, impulsive, erratic, giddy and glorious — dictated my actions.

I believed that this was the way to stand up for myself.

This made me emotive, fervent, exhausted.

Feeling indignant about one thing affected everything.

As I got older I began to understand that while emotions needed to be felt, they did not need to rule me.

I became more adroit at holding them and giving them a fair space but not center stage.

Today, I can be affected by something, even deeply affected, and not have it ruin my day (or my life). I can say, for example, *"I am stressed about work and irritated with someone I love and disappointed in a friend and happy about the fact that it's sunny and all these things coexist within a contended existence."*

Being a witness to the roller coaster of things happening inside me — rather than at the mercy of them — is one of the many, many reasons life is dramatically better now than it ever was in my twenties.

How To Stay Friends With Your Ex

Remaining friends with your ex means assuming full responsibility for the role you played in things not working out.

Blame feels like it absolves you so accountability is harder, at least at first.

It means you have given another a reason to still want you in their life even after they have seen you at your worst. Scared. Trapped. Threatened. Angry.

Unloved.

It means you have to create a few degrees of separation between how you feel and how you react to what you feel in the name of something more durable and this takes an appalling amount of work.

It means you have to lift off, like a useless scab, a lot of the protective coating of fear that makes you human *(ACK! I don't want him to be happy without me!)* to reveal the most splendid, truest part of love:

The only thing I want is for him to have anything he wants.

And thank you. Thank you for loving me.

Tease

When I was in junior high school a handful of girls had a reputation for being *calientahuevos*.

The meaning of this expression is similar to "being a tease".

The literal translation is "testicle warmer".

It's the girl willing to go pretty far but who stops short of engaging in full sexual intercourse.

The implication is that if you are going to make out then you are expected to go all the way.

Like, lest he get "blue balls", you owe it to him.

This is a horrific mindset because it takes away consent.

A woman is the owner of her body.

This means I can kiss you and not want to make out; make out and not want to have sex; have sex and not want to have sex again.

Saying no at any point is my right and anyone overriding it is committing sexual abuse.

If a girl says no and you are under the impression she can't say no because she has already done this much — or has already had sex with you in the past, or is your girlfriend — and push her into having sex this is the very definition of rape.

Just because behavior is culturally accepted doesn't make it right.

Devout Agnostic

I was raised by two strong, opinionated parents who did not believe in religion.

From a very early age I felt that something was missing.

Don't ask that I explain this because I don't know how.

I can tell you I went to houses of worship many times to look for something I did not find there.

I strived to be a good girl and I think this existential search was my only act of (unintended) rebellion.

Today, I consider myself to be a devout agnostic.

Devotion and an ability to surrender bring me supreme peace and happiness.

I am not religious. I don't know if there is a God.

For me, faith in something bigger than me is vital, essential; and an antidote to despair and darkness.

I deeply respect other people's beliefs and deeply respect my own even if I cannot (nor need to) explain them.

Beyond Literature

Jorge Luis Borges, my Dad's favorite, wrote a beautiful poem about the moon.

(Dad, thank you for reading it to me. I can still hear you.)

In this poem Borges claims there once was a master project to describe the universe, and as the finishing touches were being polished the author discovered with horror he had forgotten to describe the moon.

Since then every poet is possessed by a secret imperative to attempt to describe it.

Borges says that the moon is where our dreams live, the place where lost time goes, as well as everything both possible and impossible (which, he assures us, are the same thing).

He ends by declaring the moon is beyond his literature.

Beyond the literature of one of the best poets to ever exist.

The etymology of the word *"lunacy"* and *"lunatic"* come from *luna*, Latin for moon. It was believed that the different phases of the moon caused insanity.

I regularly moonbathe and frequently moon watch with naked eyes.

I wouldn't want to risk the pitfalls and the tedium of a sane and balanced life.

Snow Day

I have never experienced a snow day but there happens to be a strapping Canadian standing in my kitchen.

"Boyfriend, what's a snow day?"

He stops what he's doing. He turns towards the window. He looks wistful. He looks moved.

"Dushka."

"Imagine if during the week there is a snow storm. It's so thick that streets are deemed unsafe to drive."

"You would see snow falling and sit and listen to the radio listing off schools that would be closed on that day."

"The name of yours would be called."

"You'd realize you did not have to go. You'd grab your hat and gloves and run outside."

"You'd find your neighborhood friends, build snow forts for snow fights, build igloos and sled and toboggan. You wouldn't get back home until dark."

"If there was an exam on that day or you had important homework to turn in that you perhaps had not finished, this was a reprieve from the sky."

Snow days, it turns out, don't only happen on television or in Calvin and Hobbes comic strips. They are actually a thing.

Thanksgiving

I'm grateful for my family and for so many good friends who understand when I say I need to leave early.

I'm grateful for all the gifts people have given me with no intention of doing so: gifts as a fortunate side effect.

Like my brother and his wife, who in deciding to have kids made me an aunt. Like Boyfriend, who in loving to cook feeds me regularly. Like my Mom's husband, who fell in love with her and adopted her kids (even though we already had a loving Dad).

I am grateful for all the things that have been there the whole time I thought I had irrevocably lost them.

I am grateful for my body for being so miraculous (just check out your shoulder's ability to rotate and all the things your hands can do).

I'm grateful for hazelnut macaroons and any flavor, really.

I am grateful for clouds with or without grandiose formations.

I am grateful for grass when it looks mossy and soft.

I am grateful for hosts inclined to spend time on the creation of elaborate centerpieces.

I am grateful for leaves and every other perfect thing that has fallen softly from the sky and landed right in front of my feet.

Completely Different

Mom: *"Dushka, can you pass me the poppyseed lemon cake?"*

Me: *"Mom, you just said you never wanted to eat again."*

Mom: *"I'm not going to eat. I'm just going to have a bite. Everyone knows that's not the same thing."*

Rain

I am in Los Angeles today and it's been raining for over an hour.

I'm sitting in a coffee shop very close to the cash register and can hear people comment on the weather as they pay for their drink.

"This rain is such a nuisance. I was going to spend the day outside with my kids and it ruined my plans."

"How blessed are we to get this refreshing rain! It's been so hot and dusty!"

"Wow! What a miracle rain is! I pray for rain every day after two years of drought!"

"This rain. Ugh. It's snarling traffic. It's slowed everything down."

I'm fascinated by what each person brings in with them because the rain, just like the passage of time, is the same for everyone. It's neither good nor bad. It's neither cruel nor kind.

It just is and beyond that it's only what we make of it.

If You Are Sad, Be Sad

I woke up sad today. A dark weight on my chest. It feels like I have something to drag behind me when I would rather walk sprightly, unburdened.

I could ignore it but when I ignore feelings they seem to assemble inside me and plot and prepare for war.

They make strategic plans to present themselves before me all at once at the worst possible moments.

I really don't want to burst out crying in the middle of a presentation.

I don't want to fight with Boyfriend over something that doesn't matter.

I do what I always do when I have feelings I need to sort out.

I set time aside to do nothing.

So, what is this? I have felt this way before.

Finally it hits me. My father died in December. I don't immediately associate the date with the anniversary of his death but my body does.

And today is December 1st.

I could fill my days with work and friends and fake holiday cheer to distract me from myself but as counterintuitive as it might seem I'm just going to stay home and be sad.

Feelings, like waves, relentless, powerful, intractable, need space to arrive and swell and retreat.

I have learned it's much better to give them what they need.

What Once Threatened Me

For me writing is a form of expression but also a form of therapy.

If I have something to sort out or process I write it down.

I let my emotions dictate the words, not my inner editor. (She can be really nosy and persistent so I gently push her out and close the door.)

Whatever is troubling me gets poured out as it comes. (She knocks a few times, gives up.)

The grimy spill of an overturned bucket sloshing with anger or frustration or incomprehension or loneliness eventually runs clean, becomes a tidy story with a glossy ribbon running through it.

My feelings and thoughts, in order, neatly wrapped.

The fact that I have articulated something makes me feel I've clasped it.

Because it's been transcribed from my heart (or my guts) to the page, the inclination to obsessively turn it over and over in my head stops.

The brain-rattling stops.

The anxiety subsides.

Then I am ready to talk. Or, talk to myself.

Or crush up what I've written and toss it across the room and into the waste basket (with my left hand and infallible aim).

This is how something that once threatened to overwhelm me ends up a crumpled up piece of paper at the bottom of a garbage can.

This Is How I Remember It

I understand intellectually that memory is a slippery thing.

I remember poems teachers asked me to recite when I was seven and they come out of my mouth decades later intact and exactly the way they were written.

I remember the page number they were on.

And yet I recall incidents and grown-ups who were at the scene protest.

"But, there was blood. I remember blood."

"Dushka. That is not exactly how it happened."

Tell me. If I can't trust my own memory, what can I trust?

Not trusting how I remember things is synonymous with not trusting myself. I would not double-cross me.

My brain does not betray itself.

I was there. I know what I saw.

I suppose my memory does the best it can. I feel I will lose my footing if I don't defend it.

I respect if you have another version of that (by logic, also imprecise).

But this is how I remember it.

My Elevator Buddy

I was dashing to catch the elevator and when I did I realized there was a guy already inside holding the door open for me.

"Thank you so much for waiting," I said.

"I can't decide if I should try to catch a bus from here, or an Uber." (This was me being chatty and mostly talking to myself.)

He nodded politely and stepped aside to again hold the elevator door for me. I walked out to find Boyfriend waiting in the lobby.

"Bye!" I said. *"Thank you for being such a gentleman!"*

"Dushka," Boyfriend said. *"You have no idea who that was, do you?"*

"No, but it's not the first time we shared an elevator and he is unfailingly kind. Mark my words. That's one good guy."

Boyfriend stops, looks something up on his phone and holds it up so I can see the photo on his screen.

"Hey!" I say. *"My elevator buddy!"*

"That," he says *"was Dustin Moskovitz."*

Beginner's Mind Forever

Amateur is such an interesting word.

An amateur is a person who engages in something because they like it and not because they intend to get paid for it.

Or, a person who admires something and devotes time to it for fun (an amateur of the theater).

It also means someone who lacks experience or skill.

The origin of the word is absolutely delightful: it comes from the Latin *amatore,* lover, and refers to someone who engages in an activity for love and not for money.

The word suits me so very much, for two reasons.

The first, because I am motivated by doing what I love more than I am motivated by the notion that I will get paid for it.

The second, because I adore the Zen Buddhist notion of "shoshin", beginner's mind. Whenever I consider myself already knowledgeable or already an expert it closes me off (*"oh, I already know that."*). When I remind myself I am inexperienced it opens my mind but it also invites in wonder and adventure.

I hope to always regard the world like a beginner.

It is for all these reasons that I consider myself to be an amateur writer, and the reason why my second book is called "Amateur: an inexpert, inexperienced, unauthoritative, enamored view of life."

If someone asked me to describe myself with just two words, "amateur writer" is what I would say.

Ladybug Reunion

Today I decided to come back into my apartment building via the back door.

As I opened the gate into the patio I saw a woman and a little girl crouching by a bush, looking at something.

I thought about running on by, but decided to stop and investigate.

"Look!" The little girl said. *"Look!"*

As I got closer to the bush I saw it too.

Dozens of ladybugs poised on the leaves.

"It's the annual ladybug reunion!" I told them.

"Ladybugs are good luck," said the little girl. *"We can make thousands of wishes!"*

If it wasn't for serendipity, I would have missed my chance at a thousand wishes.

I never would have known about the annual ladybug reunion.

Monogrammed Bath Robes

One day I told Boyfriend, mostly in jest, that now that we were living together we urgently needed to get matching, monogrammed bath robes.

He looked absolutely appalled.

Then he got us matching, monogrammed bath robes.

We lounge in them.

Fattening

If you tell me I can't eat something, eating it is all I can think about.

"A paleo diet is so good for you" becomes me dreaming about toast.

If you declare I have to eat less, I get hungry. I think my body knows that there will be a food shortage and begins to conserve more energy and demand more peanut butter cookies.

So please. Abstain from uttering the word "diet" anywhere near me. It makes me fat.

No Plans

Yesterday I spent time with a beloved friend.

Our schedules are not always compatible so we don't hang out very often.

The best part is we had no specific plans.

We quaffed chai, strolled around the neighborhood, sat down to a leisurely lunch, sauntered around window shopping and chatting and wandered up and down Clarion Alley.

Then we went searching for a cookie and sat outside.

It has been much colder than usual so as I sat there in a bone-warming patch of sun with my wonderful friend, my cookie, a hot drink and nowhere to go, I felt like I had everything.

Part Fish

It takes a fraction of an instant for a child to fall into a swimming pool.

This notion terrified my parents.

"We will be hyper-vigilant," my father vowed. *"We will never take our eyes off her."*

"There is only one way to keep her safe," my Mom said. *"As early as possible she will learn to swim."*

This is how I was taught to swim before I learned to walk.

I would crawl to the edge of the pool, stand up and dive in, arms extended and pressed against my ears, head slightly tucked in.

Then, I'd swim freestyle across the length of the pool.

Soon after that I could make that trip underwater, without coming up for a breath.

My family had a place on the Pacific Coast, in what was then the very small town of Puerto Vallarta. I swam in pools and in the open ocean.

I was in the water so much the skin on the tips of my fingers shriveled and my hair never had time to fully dry.

My father used to tease me that I was part fish.

Today, I find solace in water. I move easily underneath the surface, open my eyes and delight in the blurry outlines, the light and shadow and the pattern of my own bubbles.

There is a different kind of silence there, removed and muffled; a peaceful bobbing and suspension that pushes everything else away.

Swimming is a primal joy and along with other priceless things like tirelessness, the English language, and big hands, it's one of the best things my mother gave me.

How To Eat

When we first started dating Boyfriend and I went to a ramen place we had been told was excellent.

Soon after ordering, they set before us two large, noodly, salty bowls of steaming deliciousness.

I would dunk my big spoon in and put in my mouth whatever came out. I left for the end the juicy hunks of food that were too unwieldy to end up on my spoon.

Boyfriend held the big spoon still with his left hand and dipped it gently in the piping hot broth.

With the chopsticks in his right hand he would strategically grab and place carefully chosen morsels of the ramen onto the spoon, so every single spoonful contained everything in his bowl.

A small chunk of meat, a bit of egg, some greens, and finally a long noodle, pulled out high and then lowered, curled and heaped onto the very top.

Then he'd place the spoon into his mouth.

It took five or six carefully constructed bites for him to voice his verdict.

"Hmmm. This place does have really good ramen."

317

Now, whenever we go out to a restaurant and I ask if I could please have a taste of what he ordered (which is always) he says *"hold on."*

Then he proceeds to assemble a bite for me following this same methodology.

He slices a particularly crispy and golden piece of the oven roasted chicken, for example, and spears it with his fork. Then he drags it generously across his plate to collect the herby reduction it's resting on, uses his knife to spread a pat of mashed potato on it and finally adds a bit of broccoli to the tip of the fork.

"Here you go."

As I lean in, open my mouth, then slowly chew, he assures me this is how every dish was intended to be eaten.

Still Useful

A woman with three small children gets on the bus.

She tells the driver, in Spanish, where she wants to go and the driver tries to tell her, in English, where to get off but she doesn't understand.

She seems at the end of her rope. The kids cry and pull on her. She looks increasingly distressed.

I'm about to jump in, and at that same moment the driver uses the loudspeaker.

"Does anyone here speak Spanish?"

I step forward.

My imaginary cape flaps behind me.

The driver tells me where she needs to get off and I translate, then explain to her in what direction she needs to walk once she exits the bus.

When we arrive at her stop I confirm she needs to go, then point her in the right direction.

When someone yells *"Is there a doctor in the house?"* it will never be me but I like to think that despite my limitations I can still make myself useful.

They Already Know

One of the things I remember most clearly from my childhood is how much adults revealed in my presence, talking to each other as if I was not there.

Today, I tell grown-ups that kids miss nothing. They know when you are tired. They know when you fight. They know all about whatever secrets you think you are keeping from them.

Kids are not only alarmingly sagacious. They are completely tuned in.

I know this because I remember.

You can't shelter your kids. They already know.

How Do You Respond To Criticism?

When I was about 14 years old I participated in a story writing contest organized by my school and won.

When the winner was announced, I went up on stage to receive my writing trophy. What made me happiest was that people would be proud of me.

Instead they were cruel and said mean things which took me completely by surprise.

My heart was broken.

When my Dad came into my room to congratulate me I was crying. I told him I didn't want to write anymore. I vowed I would never participate in a contest again.

"Dushka," he said, *"there are two kinds of people in the world.*

The ones that sit on the sidelines doing nothing other than finding fault with what the participants do.

And the participants.

Being a participant means having passion, being involved, taking risks, being vulnerable, being exposed and being criticized.

The more you participate the more you live.

And the more you will be a target for criticism.

Participate anyway.

When someone is particularly critical take a good look at them. Identify them. A doer, or a sideliner? When doers provide feedback, they may have a point.

Sideliners don't get to have a say. Don't listen to them.

Sideliners don't count."

Then he walked me over to his library and reached to the wall by his desk.

He took a framed quote off the wall.

"Here," he said.

"Dushka." He kissed my forehead.

"I never again want to hear you aiming to be a timid soul."

This is the quote he gave me:

"It is not the critic who counts; not the man who points out how the strong man stumbles, or where the doer of deeds could have done them better. The credit belongs to the man who is actually in the arena, whose face is marred by dust and sweat and blood; who strives valiantly; who errs, who comes short again and again, because there is no effort without error and shortcoming; but who does actually strive to do the deeds; who knows great enthusiasms, the great devotions; who spends himself in a worthy cause; who at the best knows in the end the triumph of high achievement, and who at the worst, if he fails, at least fails while daring greatly, so that his place shall never be with those cold and timid souls who neither know victory nor defeat."

— Theodore Roosevelt

Survivor

"I am a survivor. I make do with whatever resources are available."

Boyfriend, pouring eggnog into his coffee because we are out of milk.

Persistent Search

His eyes were blue and once when he was kissing me I saw something in them that frightened me.

There was love there, and giddiness and lust.

But also steadiness, unwavering.

Where I come from there was a script I was expected to follow.

The woman wants a guy to commit and the man doesn't want to and she cajoles and finds a way and he gets entangled and ultimately trapped.

This is when he proposes. Finally.

I had no precedent for what was happening here. Him, certain and true and "ready", and me, longing for who knows what that couldn't be found anywhere near here.

I said no and left and set a pattern. Whenever I reached a stable point I would flip everything over and begin again.

Through the years I never stopped thinking about him.

I finally realized it was not him I was having trouble getting over but the part of me that would have been if I had made a different decision.

He represented a safe, quiet place to set myself down.

I am more alive when I am not comfortable.

This is what I contend with. It was never him but rather my persistent search for inner peace paired with my aversion to it.

Lonely Water

In Spanish, plain water (no ice) is "agua sola".

"Sola" is also the word for "alone".

My bilingual niece requests "lonely water" before she goes to bed.

Plastic Dolls

In Mexico on January 6 we celebrate *Dia de Reyes* to honor the day the Three Wise Men gave gifts to Jesus Christ.

Dia de Reyes is a bit like Christmas. It's clearly a religious holiday but it transcends religion to become more of a cultural tradition.

On *Dia de Reyes* you sit around the table with your family or your friends and slice up a *Torta de Reyes*, a big, round bread that looks a wreath.

The baker hides a plastic doll inside the bread, and as it's sliced up and shared someone gets the slice with the doll in it.

When you're little, getting the doll is the dream.

When I was a kid a friend of mine cried inconsolably because she wanted the doll to be in her slice and it wasn't.

Her father, wanting to give her everything she wanted, went to a store and got a big bag of plastic dolls and gave them to his daughter that evening.

Getting a big bag filled with dolls was nothing like getting it in the slice. It was nothing like not knowing who was going to find it. It was nothing like sinking the fork into your slice to feel something hard and unyielding and realizing it was you and shrieking and raising your plate for everyone to see.

He ruined it for her.

Never hand yourself — or anyone else — a big, meaningless bag of plastic dolls.

Why would you want to ruin things?

Impossible Balance

My Dad died December 15, 2014.

Other people wear black as a sign of mourning. My body refuses to acknowledge the existence of Christmas.

This year I had many different options available to me on December 25 and I just did not feel like saying yes to any of them.

My friend Amit was the most adamant on not allowing me to spend the day alone. *"But Dushka, please! This makes no sense! Be reasonable! Why would you want to be alone on Christmas?"*

I finally persuaded him to proceed with his merry plans and let me be.

95% of the time I'm happy when I'm alone.

The other 5% I am trapped in a distressing place: I don't feel at all like being in the company of others, and being alone feels wretched.

If during these times I push myself and go out I wonder what on Earth I'm doing there, anywhere, with anyone, and please, I just want to go home.

If I'm home I pace and cry and ask myself what I ever did to be this lonely. *(Dushka, you just turned down at least 5 invitations, three of which involved travel with beloved family members. You did this to yourself.)*

Sometimes being an introvert requires a balance impossible to strike.

Or maybe this bleak, infrequent limbo is just me.

Good Boy

Boyfriend and I are at a bakery.

A woman walks up to the storefront and ties her big German Shepherd to a bench outside.

From the frame of the door the German Shepherd looks longingly at the bread. His eyes fall upon the fresh baked dog treats in the corner. He stares at his owner, stares at the treats.

Owner: *"Have you been a good boy?"*

Me: *"HECK YA I'M AN AWESOME BOY!"*

Owner: *"Do you want a treat?"*

Boyfriend: *"I'M THE BEST DAMN BOY YOU'VE EVER SEEN!"*

Clearly we have a brilliant future as dog interpreters.

Our Own Universe

I was at a restaurant having dinner and the two people sitting right next to me were arguing about what they were eating.

"Wow. This is really spicy."

"No it isn't! It's perfect!"

"It's burning my mouth. I can't even eat anymore."

"It's so delicious."

They were eating off the same plate, putting the same food into their mouth and experiencing completely different things.

This is just two people and a discrepancy in a sense of taste.

Take that and throw at it the inevitable complexity of our condition.

I think we all live in our own universe and the fact that we even believe we are communicating is nothing short of a miracle.

Hard And Fast

I am writing something introspective and as a result am completely absorbed in my device as I step into the elevator.

"I will work hard and fast to get rid of all your squeaks and grinds," a gruff voice says.

I jump ten feet before realizing the guy talking is the elevator repairman.

Why Did You Bring Me Into The World?

My Mom used to ride horses.

One day her horse spooked and she yanked on the reins, accidentally pulling the horse on top of her.

She was in the hospital for weeks, with multiple injuries and a pelvis fractured in five different places.

She was told she would never walk again, and that she could not have children.

When she married my father they tried everything and could not conceive.

One day, there I was.

Whenever I asked my mother why she brought me into the world, or told her I didn't ask to be born, she would laugh.

"You fought tooth and nail to be here. You clawed your way into the world with unstoppable force."

"After years of trying, after giving up, the doctor performed an ultrasound and we heard your heart beat so sure and strong."

"When you were in my belly you'd wake your father up with your kicking."

"You are here because you demanded it."

"Trust me, Dushka. We were just your means of transport."

I had no idea what to reply to this, mostly because I knew in my bones that it was the truth.

My Favorite Person

My favorite people defy convention. They were always told to do things a certain way and found their own way. Not necessarily as a form of rebellion but rather in an honest, curious, often painful search for identity and happiness.

They have courage. I like people who speak up and who stand for something, who take a side; who challenge ordinary thinking without really intending to.

My favorite people are accidental revolutionaries.

They do things wholeheartedly. By extension I really dig passion, discipline, dedication, determination.

Competency in any form makes me weak in the knees.

I have nothing against sarcasm but I think it's unfortunate that it's so often mistaken for intelligence. I would rather marvel in what someone is saying than expend energy trying to figure out what they really mean.

I find virtue — trying to do the right thing — decency and kindness endlessly interesting because we are all intensely flawed so there is an inherent, textured struggle in trying to be good.

I love it when my eyes are suddenly opened in a way that makes me realize I have been wrong, like I unwrapped something resplendent and clarifying.

This feels less like *"you are wrong"* and more like looking at a wall and being turned towards a window with a beautiful view. *"Look, see? See how clear it is if you look at it this way instead?"*

Thank you, favorite people. Thank you for existing.

How Do You Keep Quora Fame From Going To Your Head?

When Boyfriend tells me I'm terrible at loading the dishwasher and gently pulls everything out and places it back in gorgeous, symmetric rows I tell him I might suck at this but that there is a place where I am famous.

Famous, I repeat.

He rolls his eyes.

When I call my Mom and tell her what Quora is, what an upvote means, she tells me that this to her makes perfect sense.

Then she reminds me that ever since I was a little girl I always had imaginary friends.

I call my brother to explain. Before I can say anything he tells me his daughter told her friends at school that her Dad is a superhero who hides his costume in the back of his closet.

I walk the world with my Quora t-shirt and my Quora bag and think *I am a Top Writer. I am a Top Writer, and nobody knows.*

It stands to reason that others hold secrets too.

I bet you I walk among royalty. I am surrounded by heroes, by emperors, by warriors, by adventurers and demigods.

We are, each of us, the ultimate legend to the people who love us.

Everything else is just a mirage.

About the Author

After more than 20 years in the communications industry I noticed a theme.

It is very difficult to articulate who you are and what you do.

This holds true for both companies and for individuals.

For companies, this is an impediment to the development of an identity, a reputation, a brand.

It makes it hard for your customers to see how you are different from your competitors.

For individuals, in a new world order of personal brands, it makes it hard to develop one that feels real.

This is what I do. I help companies and people put into simple terms who they are, what they do, and where to go next.

My work comes to life through message development, presentation training, media training and personal brand development.

It comes to life through executive coaching, workshops and public speaking.

It comes to life through what I write.

My first book is called "How to be Ferociously Happy", "Amateur" is my second, and "A Spectacular Catastrophe and other things I recommend" is my third.

I live in San Francisco with Boyfriend, who snores like a cartoon bear.

Made in the USA
San Bernardino, CA
13 November 2017